Haggai, Zechariah, and Malachi
An Introduction and Study Guide

T0285017

T&T CLARK STUDY GUIDES TO THE OLD TESTAMENT

Haggai, Zechariah, and Malachi
An Introduction and Study Guide
Series Editor
Adrian Curtis, University of Manchester, UK
Published in association with the Society for Old Testament Study

OTHER TITLES IN THE SERIES INCLUDE:

T & T CLARK STUDY GUIDES TO THE NEW TESTAMENT:

Haggai, Zechariah, and Malachi
An Introduction and Study Guide

Return and Restoration

By
Michael R. Stead

t&t clark
LONDON • NEW YORK • OXFORD • NEW DELHI • SYDNEY

T&T CLARK
Bloomsbury Publishing Plc
50 Bedford Square, London, WC1B 3DP, UK
1385 Broadway, New York, NY 10018, USA
29 Earlsfort Terrace, Dublin 2, Ireland

BLOOMSBURY, T&T CLARK and the T&T Clark logo are trademarks
of Bloomsbury Publishing Plc

First published in Great Britain 2022

Cover design by clareturner.co.uk

A catalogue record for this book is available from the British Library.

Library of Congress Control Number: 2021945652

ISBN: HB: 978-0-5676-9943-5
         PB: 978-0-5676-9942-8
         ePDF: 978-0-5676-9945-9
         eBook: 978-0-5676-9946-6

Series: T&T Clark's Study Guides to the Old Testament

Typeset by Integra Software Services Pvt. Ltd.
Printed and bound in Great Britain

To find out more about our authors and books visit www.bloomsbury.com
and sign up for our newsletters

Dedicated to Felicity, Calvin, Verity, and Nathaniel.

Contents

List of Figures

Series Preface

How can a potential reader be sure that a guide to a biblical book is balanced and reliable? One answer is, "If the Guide has been produced under the auspices of an organisation such as the Society for Old Testament Study."

Founded in 1917, the Society for Old Testament Study (or SOTS as it is commonly known) is a British and Irish society for Old Testament scholars, but with a worldwide membership. It seeks to foster the academic study of the Old Testament/Hebrew Bible in various ways, for example, by arranging conferences (usually twice per year) for its members, maintaining links with other learned societies with similar interests in the British Isles and abroad, and producing a range of publications, including scholarly monographs and collections of essays by individual authors or on specific topics. Periodically it has published volumes seeking to provide an overview of recent developments and emphases in the discipline at the time of publication. The annual Society for Old Testament Study Book List, containing succinct reviews by members of the Society of works on the Old Testament and related areas, which have been published in the previous year or so, has proved an invaluable bibliographical resource.

With the needs of students in particular in mind, the Society also produced a series of study guides to the books of the Old Testament. This first series of Old Testament Guides, published for the Society by Sheffield Academic Press in the 1980s and 1990s, under the general editorship of the late Professor Norman Whybray, was well received as a very useful resource, which teachers could recommend to their students with confidence. But it has inevitably become dated with the passage of time, hence the decision that a new series should be commissioned.

The aim of the new series is to continue the tradition established by the first series, namely to provide a concise, comprehensive, manageable, and affordable guide to each biblical book. The intention is that each volume will contain an authoritative overview of the current thinking on the traditional matters of Old Testament/Hebrew Bible introduction, addressing matters of content, major critical issues, and theological perspectives, in the light of recent scholarship, and suggesting suitable further reading. Where appropriate to the particular biblical book or books, attention may also be given to less traditional approaches or particular theoretical perspectives.

All the authors are members of the Society, known for their scholarship and with wide experience of teaching in universities and colleges. The series general editor, Adrian Curtis, taught Old Testament/Hebrew Bible at the University of Manchester for many years, is a former Secretary of the Society, and was President of the Society for 2016.

It is the hope of the Society that these guides will stimulate in their readers an appreciation of the body of literature whose study is at the heart of all its activities.

1

Historical Background to the Postexilic Prophets

1.1 The Theological Expectations Arising from the Exile

Haggai, Zechariah, and Malachi are addressed to those living in Jerusalem in the early Persian period. Although written to the situation after the return from exile, these books cannot be properly understood apart from the theological expectations shaped by the exile. Not everyone had been taken into captivity (Barstad 1996), but the future hopes for the people of God rested with those who had been taken, not those who had remained (cf. Jeremiah 24).

There are ongoing debates about whether the *formative* period for the biblical texts was preexilic (e.g., Schniedewind 2004), exilic (e.g., Albertz 2003), Persian (e.g., Davies 1992, 1998), or Hellenistic (Lemche 1993). This study guide assumes that, by the end of the exile, it is likely that many of the elements of what we now know as the Hebrew Bible were beginning to take shape. This would have included (some form of) the Pentateuch, a version of what scholars call the Deuteronomistic History (a theologically shaped history that explains Israel's possession of the land as a term of God's covenant with them and expulsion from the land as the result of their covenant unfaithfulness), a collection of psalms shaped by similar themes, and a corpus of prophetic works that pronounced Yahweh's judgment on sin and promised hope beyond the judgment of exile. (This is a reasonable assumption, given the many allusions to such texts that appear in Haggai and Zechariah 1–8.)

The following passages provide a sample of these key themes.

- Deut. 29:9–30:10 (the terms of God's covenant with Israel)
- 2 Kgs 24:1-4, 18-20 (exile because of covenant unfaithfulness)

- Lamentations 3 (a "theological" account of the experience of exile)
- Jer. 30:1-22 (the promise of restoration after exile)

As a result, there was a theologically driven expectation that the exile would eventually come to an end, which Yahweh would bring his people back to their land and that there would be a restoration of all that had been lost—a rebuilt Jerusalem, a reconstituted priesthood, a reconstructed temple, and a reestablishment of the Davidic monarchy. Haggai, Zechariah, and Malachi address, in different ways, those whose experience of return failed to live up to their expectations of the glorious restoration envisaged in the prophets.

1.2 A Caveat about Sources and Unresolved Historical Questions

The following account of the history of the postexilic period has been reconstructed from a variety of sources. There are tensions (and in some cases inconsistencies) between data from documentary sources (both biblical and extra-biblical) and archaeological data.

There is an ongoing debate between what has been dubbed a "maximalist" approach (which presumes the historical veracity of the biblical texts, unless proven otherwise) and a "minimalist" approach (which presumes the historical unreliability of biblical texts, unless independently confirmed). This study guide will seek to take a middle path, by using the documentary sources to reconstruct a history, while at the same time highlighting the key tensions and unresolved historical questions.

On the reliability of Ezra-Nehemiah as a historical source, see Williamson (1983, 1985:xxviii–xxxii) for one view and Grabbe (2006) for the counterview. For a summary of the tensions between Ezra-Nehemiah and a historical reconstruction, see Grabbe (2015).

1.3 Under Persian (Achaemenid) Rule

The military conquests of Cyrus II (Cyrus the Great) established the Persian (Achaemenid) Empire. The Achaemenid Empire takes its name from Achaemenes, who was (according to Darius) the common ancestor of both Cyrus the Great and Darius (see Figure 1.1 for the family tree of the Achaemenid dynasty).

Cyrus the Great rose to prominence around 550 BCE, after defeating the Medes and winning a series of victories over Babylonian forces in Asia Minor. After routing the Babylonian army at Opis, Cyrus was able to capture the city of Babylon largely unopposed in October 539 BCE (Briant 2002:41–4).

Cyrus's victory is celebrated in a cuneiform tablet known as the Cyrus Cylinder, which attributes the defeat of the Babylonian king Nabonidus to the judgment of Marduk, the patron deity of Babylon. Lines 28–33 describe how Cyrus restored the cultic items that had been captured by Babylon to their native temples and returned captives to their native lands, directing that prayers be offered for Cyrus. The message on the cylinder is focused to the East of the Tigris River, and as such the Jewish people and religion are not explicitly referenced. However, the policy of repatriation and recommissioning of worship at local temples is *broadly* consistent with the terms of Cyrus's edict as recorded in the Hebrew Bible (cf. Briant 2002:46–8).

Cyrus receives positive treatment in the biblical texts. He is described as Yahweh's anointed in Isa. 45:1, and accounts of his edict are recorded in Ezra 1:1-4, 6:1-5, and 2 Chron. 36:22-23. In the biblical account, Cyrus is integral to Yahweh's plan to bring his people back "when the 70 years of Babylon are complete" (Jer. 29:1-14, cf. Isa. 44:28).

1.4 The First Return under Sheshbazzar

In response to Cyrus's edict in 538 BCE, a first wave of Israelites returned to Jerusalem. According to Ezra 1:5, this group was under the leadership of Sheshbazzar, who is described as "the prince of Judah" and comprised the "family heads of Judah and Benjamin and the priests and Levites." The retrospective account of this period in Ezra 5:14-16 indicates that Cyrus had appointed Sheshbazzar as governor (perhaps a Neo-Babylonian carryover appointment—see Silverman 2015), given him articles of gold and silver that had been taken from the Jerusalem temple, and commissioned him to rebuild the temple in Jerusalem.

Scholars are divided over how to correlate the historical data in Ezra 1–6 with Haggai and Zechariah. This study guide follows Williamson (1983: 16–20) and interprets Ezra 1 as describing the first wave of returnees under

Sheshbazzar after Cyrus's edict in 539 BCE (about which Ezra 5:13-17 provides an historical retrospect), and Ezra 2–6 as describing the activities of a second wave of returnees led by Zerubbabel and Joshua, who are active in Jerusalem early in the reign of Darius, and thus that the refounding described in Ezra 3:10-13 is the same event alluded to in Hag. 2:18. Ezra 4:6-24 interrupts the chronological sequence by recounting stories of later opposition in order to demonstrate that the resistance to rebuilding the temple was also later manifest in opposition to the rebuilding of the walls and city of Jerusalem.

Haggai and Zechariah 1–8 make no reference to a prior laying of the temple's foundations in the time of Sheshbazzar (cf. Ezra 5:16). Work on the temple evidently did not progress very much between 538 and 520 BCE, because Hag. 1:4 (*c.* 520 BCE) describes the house of Yahweh as still being a "desolation."

It is not clear how large either contingent of returnees was. Although there are divergent views (e.g., Hill 2012:33), the view taken here is that the list of returnees in Ezra 2 relates to a second contingent who returned circa 520 BCE with Zerubbabel and Joshua (or perhaps the total of both contingents).

Either way, the number of the returnees in Ezra 2 (*c.* 50,000) is in tension with archaeological population estimates, which indicate that the entire population of Judah in the early Persian period was no more than 30,000, with the initial population in Jerusalem up to 3,000 persons (Grabbe 2015:294–5, cf. Carter 1999).

1.5 The Rise of Darius

There was considerable political turmoil surrounding the rise of Darius in the two years immediately preceding the recommencement of work on the Jerusalem temple in 520 BCE. One source of information about this is the Behistun Inscription. The Behistun Inscription is a massive stone relief and accompanying text in three languages, which Darius had carved on a cliff face of Mount Behistun in Western Iran. According to Darius's account in the inscription, Cambyses, the son of Cyrus II, who ruled from Cyrus's death in 530 BCE, secretly killed his brother Smerdis, also known as Bardiya. In March 522 BCE, a man named Gaumâta led a revolt, claiming to be Smerdis, the brother of Cambyses. Gaumâta/Smerdis seized the control of the kingdom from Cambyses, who then died of natural causes. In September 522 BCE, Darius overthrew and killed Gaumâta/Smerdis and became king.

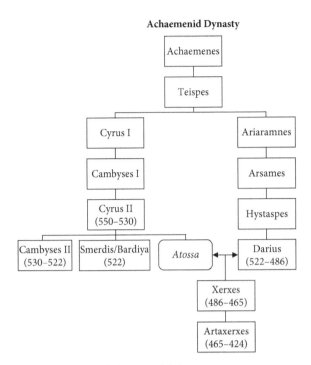

Figure 1.1 The Achaemenid dynasty

The accession of Darius occurred in late 522 BCE—perhaps December 22, though see Edelman (2005:99–103) for other options.

Darius spent the next year fighting nineteen battles to quell revolts in a number of provinces. There were also subsequent rebellions by the Elamites (*c.* 521 BCE) and Scythians (*c.* 520 BCE), which he also successfully put down. By around 520 BCE, Darius was the undisputed ruler of the Persian Empire.

In the Behistun Inscription, Darius traces his ancestry back to Achaemenes, whom he identifies as the founder of a royal dynasty that included Cyrus and Cambyses. The inscription depicts Darius's rise to the throne as a reestablishment of the kingdom that had been stolen by a usurper. Darius reinforced his claim to the throne by marrying Atossa, who was both a daughter of Cyrus and the wife of Cambyses (Herodotus, *Hist,* 3.88), and she bore him a son, Xerxes.

Darius describes himself as a restorer: "I restored that which had been taken away, as it was in the days of old" (*Behistun* line 14). He describes how he restored the kingdom, restored temples destroyed by Gaumâta, and restored people to their lands. This depiction is consistent with the account of Darius in Ezra 6:1-12.

1.6 "Yehud" under Persian Administration

According to Herodotus, the Greek historian, Darius reconfigured the Persian Empire into twenty satrapies (*Hist* 3.89). The fifth satrapy was "Beyond the River" (*ebir-nāri*), covering the region west of the Euphrates, including Syria and Palestine (*Hist* 3.91). Ezra 5:3 identifies the governor of "Beyond the River" at this time as Tattenai (who appears in cuneiform sources as Tattannu—see Rainey 1969).

"Yehud" (the Aramaic name for Judah) was a tiny sub-province of "Beyond the River" with a Persian-appointed local governor. We have only limited information about these governors. Only three are identified by name in biblical sources—Sheshbazzar, the first governor at the time of Cyrus; Zerubbabel, who was governor at the time of Darius (Hag. 1:1); and Nehemiah, who was governor during the reign of Artaxerxes I (see §1.8).

To fill in the gap between Zerubbabel and Nehemiah, Meyers and Meyers (1987:14) use bullae and seals from the early Persian period to recreate the following succession of governors of Yehud.

> * Zerubbabel (520–510?)
> * Elnathan (510–490?), whose wife was Shelomith, daughter of Zerubbabel
> * Yeho'ezer (490–470?)
> * Ahzai (470–?)
> * Nehemiah (445–433)

1.7 The Situation in Judah in 520 BCE

The year 520 BCE is the immediate context for the prophetic ministry of Haggai and Zechariah (see §2.1 and §3.1). The community were under the leadership of Zerubbabel and Joshua and had been experiencing drought and scarcity for some time (Hag. 1:6, 9-11, cf. Zech. 8:10-12).

Zerubbabel was the Persian-appointed governor of Judah at this time. Zerubbabel was the grandson of Jehoiachin, the king of Judah at the time of the exile (1 Chron. 3:19). However, unraveling the ancestry of Zerubbabel is complex. Zerubbabel is described as the "son of Shealtiel" in Hag. 1:1, 1:12-14, 2:3, 2:23; Ezra 3:2, 3:8, 5:2; and Neh. 12:1. However, in 1 Chron.

3:17-19, "Shealtiel, the son of Jehoiachin" is listed with no offspring, and instead, Zerubbabel is listed as the first son of Pedaiah, the brother of Shealtiel. The most reasonable explanations for this involve either levirate marriage or adoption. The uncertainties are compounded because the command of Jer. 22:30 to "record this man (Jehoiachin) as if childless" may have had particular implications for a genealogy traced through him.

Joshua (also spelled Jeshua) was the High Priest (lit. "Great Priest") at the time of Zerubbabel. Joshua was the son of Jehozadak (also spelled Jozadak), and grandson of Seraiah, the chief priest at the time of the exile (2 Kgs 25:18, 1 Chron. 6:15). Both Joshua and Zerubababel are central figures in the biblical accounts of the rebuilding of the temple (Haggai 1–2, Zechariah 3–6, Ezra 2–5). On the role of the priesthood in this period, see further Boda (2012), Grabbe (2016), and Redditt (2016).

The consensus view (based on Ezra 6:15) is that the rebuilding of the temple was completed in 515 BCE (contra Grabbe 2015:305, who argues that it was not finished until around 500 BCE, and Edelman 2005, who argues for a redating of the temple-building project to the reign of Artaxerxes I).

1.8 Fifth Century BCE—Darius, Xerxes, and Artaxerxes

Whereas the events around 520 BCE are the context for Haggai and Zechariah 1–8, Zechariah 9–14 and Malachi relate to a later period. There is a range of views about how much later, which will be discussed in §5.1 and §6.2. But it is likely that the fifth century BCE is the context for Zechariah 9–14 and Malachi, either during the final phase of the reign of Darius (d. 486) or the reigns of his son, Xerxes (486–465) and grandson, Artaxerxes I (465–424).

Through successful military campaigns over decades, Darius created the largest empire the world had ever known, but victory over the Greeks proved to be elusive. Although some Greek city states had come under Persian rule as early as 510 BCE, tensions simmered between the Persian Empire and Greece until it erupted in conflict in 500 BCE. Over the next decade, there were various clashes between Persian and Greek forces, with wins and losses both ways. A critical turning point occurred in 490 BCE at Marathon, when the Persian army was soundly defeated by the Athenian army. This marked the end of Darius's first Greek campaign. He retreated to prepare for a second campaign against the Greeks, which was interrupted by a revolt in Egypt. Darius died in 486 BCE before he could pursue this second campaign.

Darius was succeeded by his son Xerxes, who began his rule by putting down the revolt in Egypt and appointing his brother Achaemenes as satrap in Egypt (484 BCE). In the biblical texts, Xerxes is called Ahasuerus (e.g., Ezra 4:6 ʾăhašwērôš).

In the first years of his rule, Xerxes sought to pursue the military campaign against the Greeks started by Darius. Although there were some significant early victories (e.g., Thermopylae and Athens), the defeat of the Persian fleet at Salamis in 480 BCE and the resounding loss of the Persian army at Plataea and Mycale the following year put an end to Xerxes's military ambitions against the Greek city states (see further Briant 2002:525–49). Xerxes was assassinated in 465 BCE and succeeded by his son Arses, who took the regnal name Artaxerxes.

There are differing accounts as to how Artaxerxes came to power instead of Xerxes's firstborn son, Darius. The likely reconstruction is that Xerxes was assassinated by conspirators led by his chief bodyguard, Artabanus. Artabanus then falsely accused Darius of assassinating his father, and Artaxerxes killed his brother to avenge his father's death (see Briant 2002:563–7).

Artaxerxes ascended to the throne in 465 BCE and reigned for four decades. Like his father, Artaxerxes had to respond to challenges from both Egyptian and Greek forces in the early part of his rule. After a decade of conflict, a negotiated "Peace of Callais" (449 BCE) paused hostilities between Persia and Greece for three decades. (There are some doubts about the historicity of this peace treaty. However, it is evident that hostilities ceased around the middle of the fifth century BCE.)

The ministries of Ezra and Nehemiah occur during the reign of Artaxerxes. According to Ezra 7:7, Ezra arrived in Jerusalem in the "seventh year of Artaxerxes" (458 BCE). According to Neh. 5:14, Nehemiah was governor in Judah "from the twentieth year to the thirty-second year of Artaxerxes" (445–432 BCE).

Some question these dates for a number of reasons. For example, it is argued that Ezra, who might be expected to figure prominently in the leadership of the community, is almost absent from the "Nehemiah memoir" (but see Neh. 12:36) and that Ezra 9:9 refers to a "wall of protection" some years prior to Nehemiah's rebuilding of the walls. (For a full analysis of the points of tension, see Yamauchi 1980.)

One solution is to understand Ezra 7:7 to refer to the "seventh year of Artaxerxes II," the grandson of Artaxerxes I. On this basis, Ezra's ministry would have commenced in 398 BCE.

The prolegomenon to the 1970 reprint of C. C. Torrey's *Ezra Studies* declared that "the placing of Ezra after Nehemiah may now be spoken of as part of 'critical orthodoxy.'" Over the past fifty years, the pendulum of critical orthodoxy has swung back in the opposite direction with most scholars now no longer convinced by the argument to reverse the order of Ezra and Nehemiah.

One of the continuing debates surrounding this period is the nature and extent of possible conflicts within the postexilic community, and of conflicts with other near neighbors.

According to Ezra 3:3, the community under Joshua and Zerubbabel were afraid of "the peoples of the lands." In Ezra 4, "the people of the land" are identified as "adversaries of Judah and Benjamin" who have been worshiping God "since the days of Esarhaddon king of Assyria who brought us here" (Ezra 4:1-4). Ezra 9–10 addresses the issue of intermarriage with the "peoples of the lands."

Is this describing conflict between "Jews" and "foreigners" or between two groups of Jews—"returnees" and "remainees"? These questions are explored in Barstad (1996), Bedford (2001:270–85), and summarized in Grabbe (2004:285–8).

2

Biblical Criticism and the Postexilic Prophets

2.1 The Swinging Pendulum of Biblical Criticism

Someone coming fresh to the scholarly literature on the postexilic prophets needs to be aware of three significant "pendulum swings" in biblical criticism that have occurred over the course of the past century.

Julius Wellhausen had a profound impact on Hebrew Bible scholarship in the twentieth century, especially in the methodology of historical criticism. Wellhausen also had a particular impact on the study of the postexilic prophets. For much of the past century, the study of exilic and postexilic prophecy languished in a backwater, largely as a result of Wellhausen's views about the evolution (and devolution) of the Israelite religion. According to Wellhausen, the high-water mark of Israelite religion was the ethical monotheism represented by the preexilic prophets. Jeremiah was the last of the true prophets (1885:403–4), whereas Ezekiel was merely a "priest in prophet's mantle" (1885:59). For Wellhausen, Ezekiel and the postexilic prophets represented a regrettable descent in cultic religion and legalistic Judaism, which cast an almost century-long shadow over approaches to these prophets (see Mason 1982:137).

However, a significant turning point occurred in 1968 with the publication of Peter Ackroyd's *Exile and Restoration*. Ackroyd called for a reassessment of the exilic and postexilic prophets. Against those who had dismissed them as "not quite respectable, decadent examples of a movement now declining" (1968:xiv) and mere "background to the New Testament" (1968:2), Ackroyd argued they are integral to the theological mainstream of the Old Testament and that the exile precipitated a "creative age" for Israel, which was further interpreted in the "restoration."

In some measure due to Ackroyd, over the past four decades or so there has been an explosion of interest in the postexilic prophets, which has coincided with a paradigm shift in biblical studies generally. For most of the twentieth century, the historical critical method had been the dominant paradigm. Historical criticism seeks to explore the world "behind" the text. *Source criticism* seeks to identify the earlier sources that underlie a text and to assess their provenance and history (for a primer on Wellhausen's JEDP sources, see §6.2). *Form criticism* analyzes texts according to their genre and *Sitz im Leben* ("setting in life"). Earlier form critics presupposed that prophecy was essentially an oral phenomenon, and it was the task of form criticism to excavate a prophetic text to strip away the layers of editing in order to find the "original" message. However, the slicing and dicing of the biblical texts into *Grundtext* (the original text) and a plethora of redactional layers often resulted in a text so dismembered as to be nearly unrecognizable. *Redaction criticism* works in the opposite direction to form criticism, in that it seeks to determine how a redactor has edited and shaped sources to create a text with a view to determining the theological perspectives and/or the social conditions of the redactor.

A turning point occurred, coincidentally also in 1968, in James Muilenburg's Presidential Address to the Society of Biblical Literature, entitled "Form Criticism and Beyond." While acknowledging the importance of the historicocritical method, Muilenburg appealed for the academy "to venture beyond the confines of form criticism into an inquiry into other literary features which are all too frequently ignored today" (1969:4), which he described as rhetorical criticism. Muilenburg's Presidential Address provided a significant impetus for a variety of literary approaches to biblical texts, including post-structuralist, formalist, intertextual, reader-response, and other postmodern approaches (for an analysis of Muilenburg's impact, see House 1992:4–20). The common feature of these approaches is that the focus is on *literary features* of the *final form* of the text. The rise of these new approaches has led to a fruitful cross-fertilization between historical criticism and literary criticism. For examples of how this has benefited the study of the postexilic prophets, see Redditt (2015).

A third pendulum swing that has occurred has been in the field of textual criticism. Goshen-Gottstein (editor of the *Hebrew University Bible*) argues that there has been a "rebirth of textual criticism" (1983:386) that began in the 1950s, prompted only in part by the discoveries at Qumran. Previously, "reputable scholars were ready to jump to emendation before they gave themselves a chance to check the evidence," in part "because practitioners of biblical exegesis were not adept anymore at doing firsthand text-critical work in all areas" (1983:398). But now that there are critical editions of the Hebrew text, the Septuagint (an early Greek translation, sometimes abbreviated as LXX), the Targums (Aramaic translations), and the Peshitta (a Syriac translation), the modern biblical scholar is able to make informed exegetical choices. As a result of this "rebirth," there has been a marked swing in OT studies toward according primacy to the Hebrew text and only emending where there are compelling textual arguments with versional support.

Each of these pendulum swings has had an impact on critical approaches to the postexilic prophets, which are discussed briefly below.

2.2 The Postexilic Prophets and the "End of Prophecy"?

According to Wellhausen, Zechariah and the other postexilic prophets are not true prophets. "Zechariah speaks of the old prophets as a series which is closed, in which he and those like him are not to be reckoned" (1885:403–4). Previous generations of scholars followed Wellhausen in differentiating between the postexilic prophets and those who came before, detecting in them a profound shift in the nature of prophecy, triggered by the fall of the monarchy (Cross 1973:343), and "the radically altered setting in the post-exilic community" (Hanson 1979:10).

According to Petersen, the postexilic writers of the deuteroprophetic collections (which include Zechariah 9–14 and Malachi) believed that "[c]lassical Israelite prophecy was a thing of the past and claims for contemporary manifestations of prophecy were to be denied. The appropriate task for prophetic traditionists was not to be prophets but was instead to reflect on the earlier prophetic words and to interpret them for their own age" (1977:45). Petersen interprets Zech. 13:2-6 as a text denigrating *all* prophetic activity (not merely false prophecy), seeking "to expunge all prophets as unclean" (1977:37–8).

According to Petersen, Haggai and Zechariah 1–8 represent "a last gasp of classical prophecy" (1977:97). Bosshard and Kratz (1990:36–7) argue that the *Grundtext* of Malachi was composed as a literary continuation of Haggai and Zechariah 1–8, to explain the nonappearance of the promised salvation, by transforming their promises "eschatologisch und mit prophetischer Autorität" ("eschatologically and with prophetic authority"). Similarly, Gonzalez (2013:13) argues that Zechariah 9–14 is probably the fruit of scribal intervention, which "edited, updated, and expanded [earlier texts] in order to bring them closer to their present situation," and attached this to the figure of Zechariah, the "last prophet of YHWH" (2013:43).

Whereas earlier scholarship viewed the postexilic prophets—especially Zechariah 9–14 and Malachi—negatively, as mere (re)interpretations by "scribes" rather than the inspired words of "prophets," more recent scholarship recognizes the postexilic prophets as "scribal prophecy" (in German, *Schriftprophetie*). One of the open questions is whether these works ever existed as oral prophecy or whether they were "written prophecy" from the outset. This is one area where there has been a fruitful interchange between historical criticism and literary criticism with the extensive inner-biblical "connections" between the postexilic literature and the classical prophetic tradition being explored both from the perspectives of redaction criticism and intertextuality.

2.3 The Postexilic Prophets and the Book of the Twelve

Writing in the mid-1980s, Coggins made the following comment:

> Modern critical scholarship, with its mainly historical concerns, has almost entirely ignored any sense of a "Book" in studying the Minor Prophets. The twelve units are studied individually, usually in an assumed historical order, not of the books but of the individuals after whom they are named; and any sense of order and continuity within the collection is soon lost by this process.
>
> (1987:84)

The pendulum has since swung very much in the opposite direction. (For a summary, see Redditt 2003.) A key impetus for this change is the influential work of Nogalski (1993a, 1993b).

Nogalski argues that the Book of the Twelve as we now have it incorporates "two multi-volume collections whose common transmission predated the compilation of the Book of the Twelve. These two pre-existing corpora (literary precursors) postulated in this volume are the Deuteronomistic corpus (Hosea, Amos, Micah, Zephaniah) and the Haggai-Zechariah corpus (Haggai, Zech 1–8)" (1993a:18). What is now known as the Book of the Four came together through a series of expansions, evidenced by common literary devices and theological paradigms, to form a Deuteronomistic corpus to "document YHWH's prophetic message to the Northern Kingdom (Hosea, Amos) and the Southern Kingdom (Micah, Zephaniah) in paradigmatic fashion" (1993a:279). In relation to the Haggai–Zechariah 1–8 corpus, Nogalski argues that parts of Zech. 1:1-6 and Zechariah 7–8 were composed to relate Zechariah 1–8 to Haggai to create a single corpus. The forms of these two corpora were substantially fixed prior to incorporation into the Book of the Twelve.

Nogalski argues that "the majority of the editorial work related to the production of the Book of the Twelve occurs in [the] 'Joel-related layer.' This layer combined the Deuteronomistic corpus and the Haggai–Zechariah corpus, and it expanded upon the chronological framework supplied by these existing corpora by merging Joel, Obadiah, Nahum, Habakkuk, and Malachi into the two pre-existing corpora" (1993b:275). Malachi was composed as a conclusion for the whole "Book of the Twelve" (actually "Ten," at that stage).

Nogalski argues that Jonah and Zechariah 9–14 were the last text blocks added to the corpus to complete the Book of the Twelve (1993b:278). In part, this is based on Nogalski's observations that Jonah and Zechariah 9–14 are disruptions to the otherwise consistent pattern of "catchwords" that link the end of one book in the Twelve with the start of the next book (1993a:13–14, 20–57). The major stages proposed by Nogalski in the development of the Book of the Twelve are shown in Figure 2.1.

Theories as to the composition of the Book of the Twelve are directly relevant to our consideration of Haggai, Zechariah, and Malachi. As Nogalski (2020:69) notes, there are at least six different theories explaining the relationship between Zechariah 1–8, 9–14, and Malachi.

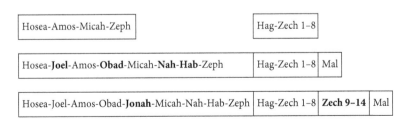

Figure 2.1 The growth of the Book of the Twelve (Nogalski)

1. Malachi was composed after and apart from Zechariah 9–14 (Hanson; Redditt).
2. Malachi followed Zechariah 1–8 as the conclusion to the Twelve prior to the compilation of Zechariah 9–14 (Nogalski).
3. Zechariah 9–14 was composed for Zechariah 1–8, but Malachi was appended to Haggai and Zechariah 1–14 wherein Malachi concluded a collection of Haggai, Zechariah, and Malachi that circulated as a separate collection (Boda; Pierce).
4. Zechariah 9–14 was added to Zechariah 8 before Malachi was appended to Zechariah 14, but Malachi already existed as a separate work (Schart).
5. Portions of Zechariah 9–14 were added to Zechariah 8 along with an existing (but not complete) version of Malachi, and both 9–14 and Malachi received additional material as part of the later editing of the Book of the Twelve (Wöhrle).
6. Zechariah 9–14 was compiled in stages to go between Zechariah 8 and Malachi (Steck).

This another field where there has been a fruitful interchange between historical criticism and literary criticism, with the textual and thematic connections across the Book of the Twelve being examined both from the perspectives of redaction criticism and intertextuality. Examples of this can be found in the various essays collected in Nogalski and Sweeney (2000); Redditt and Schart (2003); Albertz, Nogalski, and Wöhrle (2012); Boda, Floyd, and Toffelmire (2015); and Wenzel (2018).

2.4 Textual Criticism of the Postexilic Prophets

As noted above, the trend in OT studies in the last few decades is toward according primacy to the Hebrew text and only emending where there are compelling textual arguments with versional support. This reverses the pattern of much nineteenth- and twentieth-century scholarship, which was quick to accept conjectural emendations to the Masoretic Text (MT), with little or no support from the ancient versions.

The ICC Commentary on Haggai and Zechariah by Mitchell is an example of a high proclivity to emend. With reference to the Hebrew text of Haggai, Mitchell (1912:31) writes:

> [T]here can be no doubt that, like other parts of the Old Testament, it has suffered more or less in the course of the centuries at the hands of careless or ignorant readers or transcribers. Some of the resulting additions, omissions, and corruptions can easily be detected and remedied. In other cases changes that have taken place reveal themselves only to the trained critic, and by signs that will not always convince the layman.

Mitchell proposed changes in 75 percent (28/39) of the verses in Haggai (1912:32–5), 59 percent (71/121) of the verses in Zechariah 1–8 (1912:86–97), and 76 percent (68/90) of the verses in Zechariah 9–14 (1912:222–31).

The successive editions of *Biblica Hebraica*—BH³ (completed 1937), BHS (1977), BHQ (in progress)—demonstrate the trend away from conjectural emendation. For example, whereas BHS recommends forty-four changed readings (marked "l," meaning "read") to the MT of Zechariah 1–14, there are only six verses in BHQ where the preferred ("pref") reading departs from the MT.

In part, this reversal in the trend reflects a greater understanding of the textual particularities of the versions and a corresponding awareness that a variance from the MT is often not a sign that the version was translating a different *Vorlage*. (The *Vorlage* is the "prototype text" from which a translator derives a translation.)

For example, with reference to the Septuagint of the Minor Prophets, the introduction to BHQ states:

> The large majority of the differences between the two texts may be assigned to such causes as the misreading of one or more letters of the Hebrew *Vorlage*, ... differences in vocalization of the consonantal text from that found in M, and the confusion of similar verbal roots and of actual homonyms ... It seems clear that at times the Greek translators experienced some difficulty in understanding their Hebrew *Vorlage*. At some times, when the overall sense of a passage is obscure, they show a tendency to offer equivalents on a word-to-word basis, while at other times they try to make sense of the whole passage by offering a freer rendering. Moreover, they evidently felt no obligation to offer a slavishly literal translation, but rather a freedom to smooth out potential obscurities such as the change of person within a passage in order to produce a more intelligible text.

Many of the differences from the Hebrew text can be readily explained as translational adaptations or stylistic modifications.

(BHQ Minor Prophets, Introduction, p. 7)

Similarly, Gordon (1994:62) notes that the translators of the Targum to the Minor Prophets occasionally resort to paraphrase "especially when the idiom gap between the source and the target language was wide." There is "frequent recourse to 'standard' or 'parallel' translation," and occasional expansive interpretations using later techniques such as midrash. The translators have modified suffixes, changed prepositions, pluralized noun and verbs, or otherwise revocalized the Hebrew (see 1994:64–7, cf. Jansma 1950:18–23). Sometimes, the Targum "aims at replacing the metaphors of [the MT] by that to which they refer. This interpretation of [the Targum] is sometimes successful and sometimes not" (Jansma 1950:22). The analysis of Gordon demonstrates that most of the divergences between the MT and the Targum "are explicable in terms of the translation method of Tg and provide no evidence of a divergent Hebrew Vorlage" (1994:67).

The Vulgate is a translation of the MT (*c.* 400 CE) and typically follows the MT closely. According to Tov, "The Hebrew source of 𝔖 [=Syriac] is close to 𝔐 [the MT] containing fewer variants than 𝔊 [G=LXX] but more than the Targumim and 𝔙 [Vulgate]" (2001:152).

In §3.3, §4.3, §5.3, and §6.3 we will consider the relevant textual variants in more detail. In summary, however, there are very few textual variants in Haggai, Zechariah, and Malachi that warrant a departure from the textual tradition preserved in the MT.

2.5 The Approach Taken in This Study Guide

As noted above, current scholarly approaches to the postexilic prophets involve a fruitful dialogue between redaction criticism and literary criticism, with the methodologies and results of each informing the other. However, there remain differences in approach. This study guide takes an intertextual approach, which at times will differ from redaction criticism in relation to **who** created an allusion, the **function** of an allusion, and the significance of "**ungrammaticality**" in the text.

Who? Redaction criticism interprets some allusions as evidence of *redactional activity* designed to join two texts together, whereas my intertextual approach understands this to be a *literary device* used by an author to create an intertextual connection to another text. For example, Nogalski (1993a:264–6) argues that the allusions in Zechariah 8 to Haggai were *composed by a redactor* in the process of forming the Haggai–Zechariah 1–8 corpus, whereas I argue that these allusions were *created by the prophet Zechariah* to link Zechariah's message with the covenant-centric message of a prophetic contemporary (Stead 2009:240–1).

Function? For the redaction critic, some allusions have been added by a redactor to create connections and "seams" between otherwise unconnected texts. For example, Nogalski argues that the allusion to Amos 4:9 in Hag. 2:17 was added to Haggai "as part of the continuing unifying thread woven into the Book of the Twelve" (1993a:227). In contrast, I argue that the function of an intertext is the simultaneous activation of two texts (Stead 2009:131, 245), and that the prophet Haggai has alluded to Amos 4:9 because he wants the reader to interpret his words with Amos 4:9 in mind.

"Ungrammaticality?" Both approaches detect awkwardness of style and grammar but interpret this differently. For the redaction critic, this is a sign of (clumsy?) redaction. For example, Nogalski (1993a:228–9) argues that the words "the vine, or the fig-tree, or the pomegranate" in Hag 2:19 are secondary because the insertion "disrupts the syntax of this verse [because the following verb] demands a 3^{ms} subject" and that a redactor has added this to "provoke the images of Joel 1-2." In contrast, as I have argued elsewhere, an "ungrammaticality" can signal the existence of intertext. This builds on Riffaterre's concept of an "ungrammaticality"—a word or phrase that, because of its awkwardness in the present context, points to another text that provides the key to its decoding (Stead 2009:25).

In the overviews of Haggai, Zechariah, and Malachi below, I offer an intertextual reading, which highlights the significant intertexts in square brackets with bold italics—for example, *[Deut. 8:8]*. This is intended as a signal to the reader that the primary text should be read with the highlighted intertext in mind.

3

Haggai

3.1 Date

Haggai ministered in Jerusalem "in the second year of Darius" (520 BCE). There are six-date formulas in the book, three of which omit reference to the second year of Darius, though this is implied from the context.

The dates attached to Haggai's five oracles span less than four months (August–December 520 BCE). There is an overlap with the last date in Haggai and the first date in Zech. 1:1—see §4.1 for a visual representation of this.

The last (and thrice-occurring) date is also the most significant. The twenty-fourth day of the ninth month was the day that the foundation of Yahweh's temple was laid. Almost two decades earlier (538 BCE), Cyrus issued an edict allowing the captives to return from exile and rebuild the temple. Any previous work that may have been done under Sheshbazzar is disregarded, with Haggai declaring the temple still "in ruins" (Hag. 1:4; see §1.3, 1.4, 1.7). Haggai's preaching arose out of the people's failure to rebuild the temple after their return from exile.

3.2 The Prophet Haggai

The name "Haggai" (ḥaggay) is derived from the Hebrew word for a religious festival (ḥag). (See Koopmans 2017:5–9 on festivals in Haggai.) Like Habakkuk and Malachi, there is no reference to the prophet's lineage or place of origin.

Scholars speculate that Haggai may have been a "cultic prophet," given his focus on the temple and ritual purity (Tollington 1993:56–61; Grabbe

Verse	Regnal year	Date formula	Date (BCE)
Hag. 1:1	2nd year	6th month, 1st day	29 Aug 520
Hag. 1:15	2nd year	6th month, 24th day	21 Sep 520
Hag. 2:1	2nd year	7th month, 21st day	17 Oct 520
Hag. 2:10,18,20	2nd year	9th month, 24th day	18 Dec 520

1995:112–13), and that he was a recent returnee from Babylon, which accounts for the silence as to his place of origin (Meyers and Meyers 1987:8).

Outside the book of Haggai, the only references to Haggai occur in Ezra 5:1 and 6:14, and he is alluded to in Zech. 8:9. In the book, he is identified as both a prophet (*nābî'* Hag. 1:1) and Yahweh's messenger (*mal'āk* Hag. 1:13). These references, and the narrative of the book of Haggai itself, highlight what is most important about him—that Haggai was a prophet of Yahweh, whose preaching was instrumental in bringing about the rebuilding of Yahweh's temple in Jerusalem. Several of Haggai's oracles are described as "the word of Yahweh [which] came by the hand of Haggai the prophet" (1:1, 1:3, 2:1). This atypical formula ("by the hand of") highlights Haggai's role as a "messenger" of Yahweh (see 1:13 and see §3.4).

Hanson (1979:174–8) associates the prophet Haggai with the priestly hierocratic party who were primarily interested in cultic worship and opposed to the visionary program of the disciples of second Isaiah. There is no evidence in Haggai or Zechariah 1–8 of the deep divisions in the postexilic community posited by Hanson (see further Tollington 1993:53–5).

3.3 Text

The MT of Haggai is very straightforward with a single minor *ketiv/qere* on Hag. 1:8. This is where the Masoretic Text signals that what is written ("ketiv") should be read ("qere") differently.

Fragments of Haggai are found in 4QXII[b] (1:1-4), 4QXII[e] (2:18-21), MurXII (2:14-23). Based on the analysis in *Biblia Qumranica*, there are only two nontrivial variances from the MT (the spelling of Darius in 4QXII[b] Hag. 1:1, and *'l* for *byd* in MurXII Hag. 2:1), apart from plene spellings ("plene" spellings have additional consonants to indicate a vowel).

There are only a minimal number of divergences between the MT and LXX. Most can be explained as a misreading/mistranslations in the

LXX. For example, in Hag. 1:11 the LXX has "sword," which presupposes the Hebrew word *ḥereb*, whereas the MT has "drought" (*ḥōreb*). There are several periphrastic renderings, which do not change the sense (e.g., Hag. 2:1; 2:7). Two textual variants that arguably go to meaning occur in Hag. 2:17, where the LXX, Vulgate, Syriac, and Targum all include the verb "return," which is missing in the MT, and in Hag. 2:16, where many commentators and translations follow the LXX in reading the first word in the MT (mihyôtām, "from their being") as two words (*mh hyytm*, "what was to you?").

3.4 Genre and Composition

The book of Haggai uses various formulas both to introduce divine speech and within divine speech.

The **word-event formula** (*Wortereignisformel*) occurs five times, consisting of the noun construct phrase *dəbar*-YHWH with the verb *haya* followed by either "*by the hand of* Haggai the prophet" (*bəyad-ḥaggay hannābî*), which occurs in Hag. 1:1, 1:3, 2:1, or "*to* Haggai (the prophet)" (*ʾel-ḥaggay [hannābî]*), which occurs in Hag. 2:10 and 2:20. The word-event formulas in Zech. 1:1, 1:7, and 7:1 are closer in form to the second type. In four instances in Haggai (1:1, 2:1, 2:10, and 2:20), and always in Zechariah 1-8, the word-event formula includes a dating formula.

The **messenger formula** (*Botenformel*) also occurs eight times—Hag. 1:2, 1:5, 1:7, 1:8, 2:6, 2:7, 2:9, 2:11. Five times the form is "thus says Yahweh of Hosts" (*kōh ʾāmar yəhwâ ṣəbāʾôt*), and in 1:8, 2:7, and 2:9 in a shorter form. The appellation "Yahweh of Hosts" or variations occur frequently in Isaiah (sixty-two times) and Jeremiah (eighty-two times), never in Ezekiel, and dominantly in postexilic prophecy (Haggai, fourteen times; Zechariah 1–8, forty-four times; Zechariah 9–14, nine times; Malachi, twenty-four times). On the significance of this title, see Tollington (1993:65–70).

The **Divine oracle formula** (*Gottesspruchformel*)—*nəʾum* YHWH—which is literally "oracle of Yahweh" but often translated "declares Yahweh" or similar occurs twelve times (Hag. 1:9, 1:13, 2:4 thrice, 2:8, 2:9, 2:14, 2:17, 2:23 thrice). Of these, six are the long form *nəʾum* YHWH *ṣəbāʾôt* ("declares Yahweh of Hosts").

The distribution of these formulas has, in part, prompted theories about the composition of the book.

Ackroyd argued the book of Haggai consisted of "a number of oracles set in a framework of which at least some parts are the work of a compiler" (1951:174). Beuken (1967) dated this editing process to the milieu of the Chronicler.

The **editorial framework** has been identified as consisting of 1:1, 1:3, 1:12, [1:13a-14], 1:15, 2:1, [2:2], [2:4-5], 2:10, [2:13-14], and 2:20 (there are differing views about the sections marked with []). The framework includes the dating formulas, intermediary formulas (which identify Haggai as an agent of Yahweh's revelation), narratives describing the impact of Haggai's preaching, and the references to Haggai in the third person (see Middlemas 2011:145–9).

Although many scholars recognize that Haggai has some form of *editorial framework*, few are now convinced that this was added in a chronistic milieu. Mason (1977) demonstrates that many of the features that Beuken identified as "chronistic" are also found in Deuteronomistic texts and that nothing necessarily implies a late date for the framework. Kessler argues "that both the 'oracles' and the 'redactional material' in Haggai most likely have their origins in a similar setting" (2002:53). Kessler dates the main redaction of the book of Haggai as occurring before the completion of the temple in 515 BCE (cf. Meyers and Meyers 1987:xliv). Others, while accepting an early formation of the book, would also argue for some later redaction. Wolff (1988:17–20) argued that followers of Haggai compiled his prophecies into five scenes (*Auftrittsskizzen*)—(*1:2* + 1:4-11 + *1:12-13*; 2:15-19; 2:3-9; *2:11-13* + 2:14; 2:21b-23). Subsequently, "Haggai's Chronicler" relocated 2:15-19 to its present position and added word-event formulas in 1:1 + 3, 1:15, 1:15b–2:2, 2:10, 2:21a and made other changes. According to Wolff, this work was completed relatively close in time to the ministry of Haggai, and then an unknown glossator made further changes at a later time (see similarly Wöhrle 2006b). Different again is Nogalski (1993a:216–37), who argues that some parts of Haggai were added as part of its integration into the Book of the Twelve (cf. Hallaschka 2011:15, 2012).

Floyd, however, argues that we should not attempt to distinguish redactional material from source material and instead recognize narration as an editorial device in Haggai that frames composites of originally separate prophetic speech (1995:473). Floyd argues that, whereas other prophetic words have incomplete sentences as introductions, Haggai's introductions are in the form of a narrative, which encapsulates the oracle. The result is "a particular kind of story in which the prophetic revelation of messages constitutes the main narrative action" (1995:479).

In summary, then, the book of Haggai contains oracles recording the "word of Yahweh" through Haggai, his messenger, which are embedded within a narrative describing the circumstances of the oracles and the impact they had on Haggai's audience. While we may distinguish between the oracles and the "editorial framework," the oracles and narrative are a unity, and each part should be understood in relationship to the other.

3.5 The Intertextuality of Haggai

Haggai often alludes to biblical traditions rather than specific texts, which makes it difficult to establish that Haggai is invoking any particular intertext. By comparison with Zechariah 1–8, 9–14, and Malachi, there has been less scholarly focus on the text-based intertextuality of Haggai, and more focus on the reuse of traditions, such as exodus traditions, temple/glory traditions, priestly traditions, and royal/Zion traditions (see, e.g., Mason 1990:186–93, Tollington 1993, Kessler 2002:271–5, Wessels 2005).

However, although it is not always possible to identify a particular intertext, it is important to note that Haggai is full of "covenant allusions" that steep Haggai's message in covenantal overtones. These intertexts will be identified in the overview in §3.7 below with [], but it is helpful to draw them together here to demonstrate the covenant-centric nature of the message.

The description in Hag. 2:5 of the **establishment of the covenant** (lit. "the word which I cut with you") is without textual parallel, but it is a clear reference to the mosaic covenant established at Sinai (see, e.g., Exod. 24:8, Deut. 29:1). This covenant was established "when they came out from Egypt" (lit. "your coming out from Egypt"), a common phrase. However, the combination of these two ideas only otherwise occurs in Deut. 29:25, 1 Kgs 8:9 = 2 Chron. 5:10, 1 Kgs 8:21, and Jer. 31:32. Deut. 29:25 is likely to be the root to this tradition.

The **Exodus event** was the prelude to the establishment of the covenant. The destruction of chariots, riders, and horses described in Hag. 2:22 alludes to Exod. 15:1-4, reconfiguring a past victory into a pattern for the future. Similarly, the motif of Yahweh shaking heaven and earth was first used to describe what happened at the time of the Exodus (Ps. 68:8 [MT 68:9], cf. Exod. 19:18) and Conquest (Judg. 5:4), but in Hag. 2:6, 21 (as in Isa.

13:13 and Joel 3:16 [4:16 MT]) this motif is redeployed to refer to a future "shaking" of the nations.

In Hag. 1:6-11, there is a fourfold allusion to the **covenant curses** (cf. Deuteronomy 11 and 28). Similar language occurs in Hag. 2:17, but this alludes to the appropriation of Deut. 28:22 in Amos 4:9—"I struck you with blight and mildew," combined with Yahweh's message through Amos—"'You did not return to me', declares Yahweh."

Notwithstanding the fact that the word "bless" only occurs once (Hag. 2:19), the theme of the **covenant blessings** underpins Hag. 1:6-11 and 2:17-19.

The "vine, fig tree, pomegranate and olive" in Hag. 2:19 reflect the blessings due to the covenant (Deut. 8:8). In Hag. 2:19, the promise "I will bless *you*" is—surprisingly—in the singular. Yahweh speaking the words "I will bless you" only occurs in key passages where Yahweh affirms his covenant commitment to Abraham (Gen. 12:2-3), Isaac (Gen. 22:17), and Jacob (Gen. 26:3).

The threefold repetition in Hag. 1:12-14 of "Yahweh their God" (especially given that the phrase "their God" is redundant) is probably a subtle allusion to the **covenant formula**, "You will be my people and I will be *your God*" (e.g., Exod. 6:7).

Yahweh's **covenant promise** "I am with you" occurs in Hag. 1:13 and 2:4. Haggai's terminology for "with you" (*ittkem*) is unusual. Elsewhere "with you" is typically *ʾimmākem*. Amos 5:14 is the best textual parallel to the declaration in Hag. 1:13 and 2:4 from Yahweh of Hosts "I am with you." Yahweh is already present because his Spirit is "standing in the midst of the people," like the pillar of cloud in Num. 14:14 (cf. Exod. 33:10). However, Yahweh's presence will be manifest when the temple is built and "filled" by his "glory" (Exod. 40:34). Those stirred up to come and do the work in 1:14 are like the workers on the tabernacle in Exod. 36:2.

Haggai 2:10-14 is an application of the **covenant torah** in Lev. 6:25-27 [MT 6:18-20], Lev. 22:4-6, and Num. 19:11, 22 to explain the implication of the people's unclean state.

Haggai 2:23 is an allusion to the "signet ring" passage in Jer. 22:24-30, reversing the repudiation of Jehoachin as the Davidic king.

I regard the similarities between Haggai and (say) Zechariah 7–8 or the work of the Chronicler (Mason 1990:187–95) to be the result of allusions to Haggai in these texts, rather than evidence of a common editor for both works or a redactional technique to link the two books together. On Ezekiel's influence on Haggai, see Kasher (2009).

3.6 Structure

There are five discrete oracles in the book, but the first two oracles (1:2-11 and 1:13) are set within a single episode (so Verhoef 1987:43; Kessler 2002:113–14), and the final two oracles (2:10-19 and 2:20-23) are a pair that occur on the same day and describe the twin impact of laying the foundation of the temple (so Koopmans 2017:4). On this basis, I propose the following three-part structure (although noting that most scholars treat the final two oracles separately, resulting in a four-part structure).

I. **Rebuild Yahweh's House (1:1-15)**
    A. The challenge to reorient and rebuild (1:1-11)
        i. Date and addressees (1:1)
        ii. "the time has not yet come" (1:2)
        iii. "Is it time for you to dwell in panelled houses?" (1:3-4)
        iv. Two ways: your prosperity (1:5-6) OR build the house (1:7-8)
        v. Covenant curses and their causes (1:9-11)
    B. Response and result (1:12-15)
        i. Twofold Response: Obeyed and feared Yahweh (1:12)
        ii. Oracle: "I am with you" (1:13)
        iii. Result: Stirred up to work on the temple (1:14-15)

II. **The Coming Glory of the Temple (2:1-9)**
    A. Former glory and future glory (2:1-9)
        i. Date and addressees (2:1-2)
        ii. Is this temple as nothing in your eyes? (2:3)
        iii. Be strong, for I am with you (2:4-5)
        iv. Shaking the nations to fill this house with glory (2:6-8)
        v. The latter glory will be greater than the former (2:9)

III. **Restoring the Foundations (2:10-23)**
    A. Restoring blessings to a defiled people (2:10-19)
        i. Date and introduction (2:10)
        ii. Two rulings from the Priests (2:11-13)
        iii. The rulings applied to the nation (2:14)
        iv. Before stone was laid on stone (2:15-17)
        v. From this day onward, I will bless you (2:18-19)
    B. Restoring the kingship (2:20-23)
        i. Date and introduction (2:20)
        ii. Shaking heavens and earth to overthrow kingdoms (2:21-22)
        iii. Zerubbabel like a "signet ring" (2:23)

3.7 Overview of Haggai—Key Issues

Key intertexts are marked with []—see §2.5 and §3.5.

[I] Rebuild Yahweh's House (Hag. 1:1-15)

Haggai's first oracle is dated to 520 BCE—sixty-six years after the destruction of the temple, and almost two decades after Cyrus had allowed the exiles to return to Jerusalem and rebuild the temple. Like the other dating formulas, this date is with reference to a pagan king (Darius), which highlights the continuing absence of a Davidic king in Jerusalem.

The oracle is addressed to Zerubbabel and Joshua, the civic and religious leaders of the day, and through them to the community as a whole (see 1:12, where all three parties—Zerubbabel, Joshua, and the people—are explicitly named). The oracle begins with a messenger formula "thus says Yahweh of hosts." But, atypically, what follows is not Yahweh's words but what the people have been saying—that "the time has not yet come to rebuild the house of Yahweh."

Scholars speculate as to why the people were saying "the time has not yet come" (see, e.g., Bedford 2001:169-8; Kessler 2002:123–7; Assis 2007; Patrick 2008). Perhaps they believed that their current circumstances were a sign that they were still under the covenant curse because their "seventy years" of judgment had not yet run its course (see Jer. 25:11; Zech. 1:12). Perhaps they did not want to be like King David who, seeing his own house of cedar, presumed to take the initiative to build a house for Yahweh before being told to do so (see 2 Samuel 7). Or perhaps it was simply a matter of pragmatism. In circumstances where resources were scarce, were they giving priority to their own material needs? However, whatever their motives, they are exposed as false in vv. 4-7.

Their motives are exposed by Yahweh's rhetorical question in v. 4. Although they claimed "the time has not yet come," they evidently had had enough "time" to devote to their own "panelled houses" (which may—Nogalski 2011:775—or may not—Kessler 2002:128—be an extravagance). The people had been prioritizing self-interest ahead of Yahweh's house, their dwellings ahead of his dwelling.

In vv. 5-8, the people are told twice to "consider their ways." Their current ways—prioritizing their own prosperity—have, ironically, led to the opposite outcome. They have "sown much and harvested little" (echoing the covenant curse of *[Deut. 28:38]*). Instead of the covenant blessing "to eat and be full" *[Deut. 11:15]*, they eat and never have enough. Verse 6 ends with a picture that summarizes the futility of their present ways—working for wages that go into a bag that cannot contain them.

Instead, the people should consider a different way—not gathering wood to panel their own houses, but gathering wood to build Yahweh's house. As Boda (2004:92) notes, the motivation given in v. 8 is *not* the corollary of v. 6 (i.e., do this so that you will be blessed). Instead, the reason to build the house is for Yahweh's pleasure and Yahweh's glorification (see Petterson 2015:59–60 for other ways that "pleasure" and "glory" have been interpreted).

These dual motivations for rebuilding—Yahweh's pleasure and Yahweh's glory—point to the twin functions of the temple. The word translated "take pleasure" is typically associated with sacrifice—sacrifices that are acceptable to Yahweh are those in which he "takes pleasure." The preexilic prophets have declared that Yahweh "took no pleasure" in the sacrifices offered at the temple *[Amos 5:22, cf. Ps. 51:16]*. Verse 8 promises reversal—Yahweh will again "take pleasure in" their sacrifices offered at the temple.

There is a similar reversal with respect to "glory." The temple was the place where the glory of Yahweh dwelt in the midst of his people (see Ps. 26:8, 1 Kgs 8:11). However, Yahweh's glory had departed from the temple almost seventy years prior (Ezek. 10:18). But by rebuilding the temple, Yahweh would against manifest his glory there (Exod. 29:43-45).

Verses 9–11 make explicit what is implicit in v. 6—that their scarcity was Yahweh's judgment. Yahweh himself "blew away" their produce (presumably a reference to dry conditions). There is a word play in Hebrew between the word for ruins in v. 9 (*ḥarēḇ*) and the word for drought in v. 11 (*ḥōreḇ*)—because they had left his house in ruins, Yahweh had ruined their crops. They had neglected Yahweh's house because each person was (literally) "rushing to his own house"—that is, seeking after their own interests.

It is because of this that Yahweh brought scarcity upon them. As in v. 6, this point is brought home by another double echo of covenant curses from Deuteronomy 11 and 28. Their recent experience—"the heavens above you have withheld the dew, and the earth has withheld its produce"—is the covenant curse of *[Deut. 11:17]*. Similarly, their experience of a "drought on grain, new wine and oil" and on "man and beast" reflects the destruction promised in *[Deut. 28:51]* for those who disobey the covenant. The fourfold repetition of covenant curses from Deuteronomy in this oracle points to the magnitude of the error of Haggai's generation. By pursuing their own houses, they had forsaken the covenant.

Verse 12 narrates the response of the community with a change in description that reflects a change in status: "these people" have become "the remnant of the people" (contra Wolff 1988:51–2, who argues that the remnant refers to returnees from exile). The "remnant" describes those left after a time of judgment who become the focus of Yahweh's ongoing purposes for his people. Their status changed because of a twofold response—fearing Yahweh and obeying his voice. Because of this, Yahweh declares "I am with you" *[cf. Amos 5:14]*. Although failed crops seemed to say "Yahweh is against us" and the ruined temple seemed to say "Yahweh is absent from us," Yahweh declares otherwise in this oracle. The same promise is repeated in Hag. 2:4, followed by an explanation of the mode of Yahweh's presence—"my Spirit remains in your midst" (2:5).

This unit ends with Yahweh "stirring up" the people's spirit (cf. Ezra 1:1), to come and "do the work" on the house of Yahweh *[echoing Exod. 36:2]*. Three times in 1:12-14 Yahweh is described as "their God." This is a truncated echo of the covenant formula—"I will be your God" *[Exod. 6:7]*, which reflects the people's change in status. Unlike other units, this unit ends with another date formula. In response to the preaching of Haggai, the people commenced work on the temple the twenty-fourth day of the sixth month. The date formula here has the same elements as the date in 1:1 (Year-Month-Day), but in reverse order (Day-Month-Year). This literary reversal complements the theme of the chapter, which describes the reversal in the people's hearts.

[II] The Coming Glory of the Temple (Hag. 2:1-9)

This oracle addresses disillusionment in the community, less than a month after work on the temple commenced, on the twenty-first day of the seventh month (1:15). The threefold addressees of this oracle are the same as 1:12 and 1:15, indicating that the same people who had responded rightly by obeying and fearing Yahweh, and whose spirits Yahweh had stirred up to work on the temple, were now dispirited by the task ahead of them.

There were evidently some who had seen "this house in its former glory." By comparison, what Haggai's contemporaries saw before them was indeed "as nothing" (cf. Ezra 3:10-13). The temple was "in ruins" (1:4) and, although they had commenced work on the temple about three weeks prior, this was apparently only preparatory work, as they had not yet got to the point of laying the foundation or putting stone upon stone (see 2:15, 18).

In response, Yahweh tells Zerubbabel, Joshua, and the people to "be strong," to "work," and to "fear not," because as they build the temple—"I am with you, declares Yahweh of hosts," reiterating the promise of 1:13. The basis of this promise is "the covenant that I made with you when you came out of Egypt" *[cf. Deut. 29:25]*. The mode of Yahweh's presence is explained in v. 5—"My Spirit is standing (ʿāmad) in your midst," like the pillar (ʿammud) of cloud standing (ʿāmad) in the midst of the people in *[Num. 14:14, cf. Exod. 33:10]*. Implicitly, the Spirit's presence will enable them to build the temple (cf. Zech. 4:6).

According to 2:6-7 (and 2:21), Yahweh is about to do again what he did in the past. When he saved his people from Egypt and brought them into the Promised Land, Yahweh shook heaven and earth *[Ps. 68:8 (MT 68:9), Judg. 5:4]*. When he made his covenant with Israel at Sinai, the whole mountain trembled at his presence (Exod. 19:18). As the prophets have promised, Yahweh is again going to shake heaven and earth *[Isa. 13:13, Joel 3:16 (MT 4:16)]*.

This will be a final shaking ("yet once more"), which will occur "in a little while." The purpose of the shaking is "so that the treasures of all nations shall come in." Yahweh himself will "fill this house with glory." As in v. 3, "glory" here refers to the material splendor of the temple, evidenced by the "gold" and "silver" in v. 8. However, there is a double sense in which Yahweh will "fill this house with glory." Elsewhere, when Yahweh "fills" the tabernacle/temple with "glory," it is a reference to the manifestation of his presence *[Exod. 40:34]*. The outward glory of the temple is a reflection of the glorious one who dwells within (Assis 2008:592).

The oracle ends with the promise that "the latter glory of this house shall be greater than the former." It will be greater because of the universal scope of its impact—Yahweh will shake "*all* nations" and bring "the treasures of *all* nations" (v. 7). Coupled with this promise of greater glory is a promise of peace (cf. 1 Chron. 22:8-10).

[III] Restoring the Foundations (Hag. 2:10-23)

Although 2:10-19 and 2:20-23 are formally two distinct oracles, they should be understood as a coordinated unit, which describes both the immediate (vv. 10-19) and ultimate (vv. 20-23) outcomes of laying the foundation of Yahweh's temple. From the twenty-fourth day of the ninth month onward, what had been unclean and unacceptable was clean and acceptable, and what had been cursed was blessed (2:10-19), and Yahweh has declared the restoration of the Davidic monarchy (2:20-23).

Hag. 2:10-19

In a departure from the form of previous oracles, this oracle begins with Haggai asking the priests for a ruling from the law about the transmission of holiness and uncleanness. The first scenario involves "holy meat" carried in the fold of a garment. According to *[Lev. 6:25-27 (MT 6:18-20)]*, the meat of a sacrifice became holy, and whatever touched the meat (such as a garment) also became holy. The issue in the first scenario is whether the garment made holy by direct touch can pass its "second degree" holiness to other objects. The answer that the priests give is "no." Holiness cannot be transmitted to the third degree. (Note: A garment that has "second degree" holiness through direct touch is different from the garments in Ezek. 44:19, which were consecrated garments [Exod. 29:21] and therefore able to make other things holy.)

The second scenario involves someone who has become unclean by contact with a dead body *[see Lev. 22:4-6, Num. 19:11]*, and whether this defilement could be further transmitted by touch. The priests' answer, which accords with *[Num. 19:22]*, demonstrates that defilement can be transmitted by indirect contact to the third degree (and beyond), in contrast to holiness, which can only be transmitted by direct contact. Defilement is more "contagious" than holiness.

This principle is then applied by analogy to the people. "Every work of their hands" and "what they offer there" are unclean. That is, both their work on the temple, as well as the agricultural produce offered in sacrifice, is unclean because the people are unclean and their defilement is transmitted to their gifts by direct touch. The temple is meant to be the place where uncleanness could be removed, but if the temple itself was contaminated, the people were in a hopeless situation. Unclean offerings offered in an unclean temple cannot make an unclean people clean again.

Verses 15–17 invite the people to consider "How did you fare?" (following the LXX; see §3.3) before they started work on the temple. Their diminished agricultural yield was because Yahweh had "struck" them with the covenant curses of "blight" and "mildew" *[Amos 4:9, itself an echo of Deut. 28:22]* when it was dry, compounded by destructive hail in the wet season (see Exod. 9:18-26). Despite this, the people had not "turned back" (reading with Amos 4:9 and the versions; see §3.3) to Yahweh.

The critical turning point was the day when "stone was placed upon stone in the temple of Yahweh." Prior to this in Haggai, the building has been described as the "house" of Yahweh. From this point onward, it is described as the "temple." The people have now "turned" to Yahweh (cf. Zech. 1:1-6).

The significance of "foundation day" is highlighted by a threefold reiteration in v. 18—the command to "consider from this day onward" (repeating v. 15), the date (the twenty-fourth day of the ninth month, mostly echoing v. 10), and the reference to *temple*-building (see v. 15).

In v. 19 Yahweh promises that this day would mark a turnaround in the agricultural prosperity for the community. The grain crop that year (harvested in May/June) had been meager (v. 16). From that poor harvest, the next season's crop would have been sown in October and November, after the early rains had softened the ground. Thus, at the date of this oracle (December 18), the seed grain was in the ground. The answer to the rhetorical question— "Is the seed yet in the barn?"—is "no," because all (or most) of their seed had been planted for the next year's harvest (contra Floyd 2000:286–96, who take the answer to the rhetorical question to be "yes"). The community had very little to live on. It was a similar situation with the produce from their orchards. The harvest from "the vine, the fig tree, the pomegranate and the olive" *[Deut. 8:8]* had been collected as at the date of this oracle, and the situation was grim—they "have yielded nothing." But the people are given the divine assurance that this is all about to change in v. 19. "But from this day on I will bless you." The form of this blessing recalls the covenant promises to the patriarchs *[Gen. 12:2-3; Gen. 22:17; Gen. 26:3]*. Because they had turned to Yahweh, Yahweh will turn their curses into blessing. These blessings are promised to appear long before the completion of the temple in 515 BCE.

Hag. 2:20-23

Whereas the focus of 2:10-19 is "*this* day" (the twenty-fourth day of the ninth month), the focus of the second oracle shifts to what will happen "on *that* day" (2:23), when Yahweh will restore "kingdom" and "kingship" to his people at an unspecified day in the future.

This oracle is addressed to Zerubbabel, identified here the "governor of Judah" (cf. v. 23). Verses 21–22 are the prelude to the climactic promise given to Zerubbabel in v. 23.

In v. 21, Yahweh promises, "I am about to shake the heavens and the earth." This parallels the promised "shaking" in 2:6, which was to happen "in a little while." The promise to shake the heavens and the earth appears in other contexts where it describes Yahweh's end-times judgment on the nations *[Isa. 13:13, Joel 3:16]*. Here, the purpose of the shaking is to overthrow thrones and kingdoms, so that the *throne* of David and the *kingdom* of Israel may be restored. This is an outworking of the reciprocal reversal promised by the prophets—the nations brought low so that Yahweh could raise his people up and restore their fortunes (see, e.g., Isa. 52:9-10; Jer. 30:16-17; Jer. 50:17-19; Joel 3:1-2 (MT 4:1-2); Mic. 5:9; Zech. 1:18-21).

Verse 22 alludes to two episodes from Israel's history to show what Yahweh will do to the "strength of the kingdoms." As he did to Egypt in the Exodus, he will "overthrow the chariots and their riders. And the horses and their riders shall go down" *[Exod. 15:1-4]*. And, as he did to the Midianites, Yahweh will set the sword of each man against the other *[Judg. 7:22]*. This "shaking" and "overturning" will bring down other thrones and kingdoms, to bring about what is promised in v. 23.

In v. 23, Zerubbabel is identified not as "governor of Judah" (as in v. 21) but as "the son of Shealtiel," which highlights his Davidic ancestry (see §1.7). The promise that Zerubbabel will like "the signet ring" alludes to the "signet ring" prophecy in *[Jer. 22:24-30]*, where the removal of the signet ring represented Yahweh's rejection of Coniah (also known as Jehoiachin) as king, with implications for both Coniah and his "seed" (Jer. 22:30). This question left unanswered by Jeremiah 22 is whether this only applies to Coniah's direct "seed" (i.e., Shealtiel), or does it include Shealtiel's son Zerubbabel and the entire Davidic line?

There are—broadly—three ways that these verses have been interpreted, in light of the fact that Zerubbabel was not crowned as king. First, Haggai prophesied that Zerubbabel would be a Davidic/messianic king, but he was mistaken (e.g., Mason 1977:25). Second, that this (despite appearances) is not a royal promise to Zerubbabel (see, e.g., Rose 2000:231–43). Third (which is the approach taken in the study guide), that the "signet ring" prophecy in Haggai signals that the royal line of David will continue through Zerubbabel, but not necessarily that he will be crowned as king (see, e.g., Petterson 2009:63–5).

What had been lost by Coniah was not merely his individual kingship, but the dynastic succession of the line of David, the restoration of which is promised to Zerubbabel in this oracle. Yahweh's description of Zerubbabel in this verse as "*my servant*" and his words "I have *chosen* you" echo the language of *[1 Kgs 11:34]*, which describe a continuing dynastic succession "for the sake of David *my servant* whom I *chose*" *[cf. Deut. 17:15]*.

This oracle declares that Yahweh will overthrow the kingdoms and the thrones of the nations, in order to reestablish his kingdom by reestablishing the royal line of David.

4

Zechariah 1–8

4.1 Date

The three date formulas in Zech. 1:1, 1:7, and 7:1 span a period of just over two years—October 520 BCE to December 518 BCE. Whereas most other prophetic date formulas are linked to a king of either Judah or Israel, these dates are expressed with reference to the regnal year of a foreign king, Darius, whose reign commenced in late 522 BCE (see §1.5–§1.7). The three dates in Zechariah 1–8 overlap with dates in the book of Haggai.

Because of the significance of the temple in Zechariah 1–8, the other relevant date is the completion of the temple in 515 BCE. This table lists the Julian calendar equivalents for key dates in this period, and Figure 4.1 shows the spans covered by each book in a timeline format.

According to Ezra 5:1-2, the rebuilding of the temple recommenced in response to the prophetic ministry and encouragement of Haggai and Zechariah. Hag. 2:18 dates the (re-)laying of the foundation as occurring on twenty-fourth day of the ninth month (December 520), which occurs midway between the prophetic messages recorded in Zech. 1:1-6 (October 520) and Zech. 1:7–6:15 (February 519).

The dating formulae in Haggai and Zechariah 1–8 are similar, which some argue is evidence of an "editorial framework" that has been added to bind the two books together (see §3.4 and §4.4.4), or it may simply reflect Persian-period scribal conventions (Tiemeyer 2020).

4.2 The Prophet Zechariah

The name Zechariah means "Yah(weh) has remembered." It is an apt name, given that Zechariah 1–8 is the outworking of Yahweh remembering his promises to his people. The little that we know about the prophet Zechariah

Verse	Regnal year	Date formula	Date (BCE)
Hag. 1:1	2nd year	6th month, 1st day	29 Aug 520
Hag. 2:1	2nd year	7th month, 21st day	17 Oct 520
Zech. 1:1	2nd year	8th month	27 Oct-24 Nov 520
Hag. 2:10,20	2nd year	9th month, 24th day	18 Dec 520
Zech. 1:17	2nd year	11th month, 24th day	15 Feb 519
Zech. 7:1	4th year	9th month, 4th day	7 Dec 518
Ezra 6:15	6th year	12th month, 3rd day	10 Mar 515

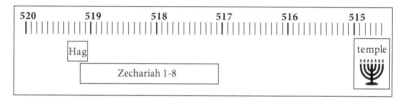

Figure 4.1 Key dates for Haggai and Zechariah 1–8

comes from inferences from Haggai, Zechariah 1–8, Ezra 2–5, and Nehemiah 12 (noting earlier caveats about these sources—see §1.2).

Zechariah is identified as the "son of Berechiah, son of Iddo" in 1:1, and the "son of Iddo" in Ezra 5:1 (there is no inconsistency here, since "son" can mean "descendant"). Nehemiah 12:4 identifies Iddo as the head of one of the priestly families that returned with Zerubbabel and Joshua, and that in the next generation, Zechariah became the head of Iddo's priestly family (Neh. 12:16). On the assumption that this pairing of Iddo and Zechariah refers to the same individuals, this means that the prophet Zechariah grew up in priestly circles, which may explain the focus on the reconstruction of the temple and the restoration of the priesthood. Zechariah is introduced in the third person in 1:1, 1:7, and 7:1, but the majority of Zechariah 1–8 is a first person account—"I saw in the night" (1:8), "Then the word of Yahweh came to me" (7:4).

4.3 Text

See general comments on textual criticism (§2.1).

The MT of Zechariah 1–8 is relatively unproblematic with minor *ketiv/qere* on only four verses (Zech. 1:4, 1:16, 2:8 [ET 2:4], and 4:2).

Hebrew fragments of Zechariah 1–8 are found in 4QXII^e (1:4–8:7) and MurXII (1:1-4), and Greek fragments in 8HevXII gr (1:1–8:22). Apart from plene variants in orthography, the only variations of substance occur in 4QXII^e at Zech. 1:6, which omits *lnw* ("[he purposed] to us"), and Zech. 3:9, which has *wmsyty* (perhaps, "and from his garment") for the MT *wmsty* ("and I will remove").

The Greek fragments of Zechariah 1–8 found at Nahal Hever (8HevXII gr) do not diverge significantly from the MT and sometimes agree with the MT against LXX—for example, Zech. 2:8.

The LXX of Zechariah 1–8 occasionally diverges from the MT, but in most cases the best explanation is not that the MT has become corrupted, but either that the LXX translator has struggled to wrestle meaning from a difficult text (e.g., Zech. 1:8, 2:4 [MT], 2:8 [MT], 4:7, 6:14, and 7:3), that the translator has provided a periphrastic or interpretative rendition (e.g., Zech. 2:8 [MT], 6:13, 8:10, and 8:21), or that the translator has misread the Hebrew *Vorlage* (e.g., Zech. 1:17, 2:17, 3:9, 5:1, and 5:3). One case where many commentators rely on the LXX to emend the MT is Zech. 5:6, amending *ʿēynām* (their eye) to *ʿăônām* (their iniquity).

The chapter division between Zechariah 1 and 2 occurs after v. 17 in the MT and LXX, and after v. 21 in the Vulgate and most English-language translations. As a result, the vision of the four horns is 2:1-4 in the MT and LXX, and 1:18-21 in the Vulgate and English versions, with a corresponding four verse offset for the balance of Zechariah 2.

4.4 Composition and Redaction History

In its final form, Zechariah 1–8 purports to record the prophetic ministry of Zechariah, addressed to those in Jerusalem between the second and fourth years of Darius (520–518 BCE). Current scholarship is divided as to whether Zechariah 1–8 is largely the product of the late sixth century BCE or whether it reflects ongoing redactions through the fifth (and perhaps fourth) century BCE. The trend in Anglophone scholarship is toward treating all or most of Zechariah 1–8 as being composed (perhaps by the prophet himself) close in time to the events it describes, with the book being edited into something like its final form around the time of the completion of the temple in 515 BCE. In contrast, the trend in continental scholarship is to treat Zechariah 1–8 as having a complex redaction history spanning a much longer period, because of what the book says about priesthood and monarchy, and because of the place of Zechariah 1–8 in the formation of the Book of the Twelve. The following paragraphs give an overview of some of the key issues in these debates about the composition history of Zechariah 1–8.

4.4.1 The Prehistory of the Visions

Were some of Zechariah's visions originally addressed to a different context? Galling (1964) argued that the first three night visions originated prior to 539 BCE with a central message about the end of the exile addressed to those in Babylon. A variation on this is Redditt, who argues that

> the original series of visions numbered seven, none of which made any reference to Joshua or Zerubbabel … The night visions were composed for Jews still in Babylon to urge them to return home and participate in God's new order … The addition of the Joshua/Zerubbabel materials (4:6b-10a; 6:11b-13; 3:1-10) provided the visions with new contents and directed them to a new audience. The new focus was the events of 520BC and the future those events were inaugurating.
>
> (Redditt 1992:255, 257)

4.4.2 The Relationship between "Vision" and "Oracle"?

A number of the visions in Zechariah 1–6 have associated oracles that report the word of Yahweh (see 1:14-17, 2:8b-17, 3:8-10, 4:6aβ-10a, 5:4, and 6:9-14).

Many scholars argue that the oracles are a later addition to the visions, to clarify or transform the meanings of the vision. However, there is no consensus as to the context or goal of this transformation. For example:

Tiemeyer (2016) argues that the visionary material in Zechariah 1–6 is the primary textual layer, and that because these visions are opaque, enigmatic, and multivalent, the oracles in Zechariah 1–8 were added relatively soon after, to clarify and delimit the meaning of the visions.

Beuken argues that the exalted role given to the priesthood in Zechariah 3 (1967:296–7) and the depiction of an enthroned priest apparently on par with a Davidic king in Zechariah 6 (1967:281) reflects a later theological viewpoint, at the times of the Chronicler.

Petersen argues that the oracles in Zechariah 1–6 "function as responses to, elucidations of, or corrections to the visions" and are more theologically conservative, in that they "soften the proposals for high-priestly authority that are expressed in the visions" (Petersen 1984:120, 125).

Meyers and Meyers argue that the oracles complement the message of the vision.

> [T]he ideas contained within the oracles amplify themes found in the visions and at the same time are based upon features of these associated visions. In other words, vision and oracle complement and supplement each other. They are alternative modes of prophetic communication, used in tandem by the prophet. Each is particularly suited to an aspect of his message, and so the message is communicated in two modes. But the message is incomplete without the mutuality of these two forms of prophetic language.
>
> (1987:lix)

My own view, similar to Meyers and Meyers, is that there is a tight integration between the visionary and oracular material in Zechariah's night visions and that each cannot be properly understood apart from the other (Stead 2014). However, to the extent that scholars read vision and oracle as having become a *literary unity* (whether or not they were a *compositional unity*), the difference between the various positions tends to become less significant.

4.4.3 Joshua and Zerubbabel in Zechariah 3, 4, and 6:9-15

One of the continuing issues of debate in relation to the redaction history of Zechariah 1–6 is focused on the Joshua/Zerubbabel materials in 3:1-10, 4:1-14, and 6:9-15. The vision in Zech. 3:1-10 is different in form from the other 7 visions (see §4.5), which is taken to be evidence that it originated from a different hand and a different context. The two oracles about Zerubbabel in Zech. 4:6-10 disrupt the vision of the lampstand in the rest of chapter, which is taken to be evidence that this too is a later insertion. The status of Zech. 6:9-15 is dependent on a prior conclusion about the timing of Zechariah 3 and Zech. 4:6-10, in that it involves two "seats/thrones," apparently one for the "Branch" and the other for Joshua.

The redaction history of this material is argued to reflect the replacement of a hope for a restoration of the Davidic monarch through Zerubbabel by an increasing centrality of the priesthood and temple. There are, however, a wide variety of explanations of both the timing and sequence of these redactions.

As noted above, Beuken argues that the exalted role given to the priesthood in Zechariah 3 (1967:296–7) and Zechariah 6 (1967:281) is a product of a later "chronistic milieu."

Jakob Wöhrle (2006a:356–66, cf. 2016) argues for a three-stage redaction. The first stage, depicting Zerubbabel and Joshua as "two sons of oil" ruling in a royal-priestly diarchy, relates to the period around the time of the completion of the temple. The Joshua Redaction (R^J) was added perhaps two decades later (late sixth century/early fifth century BCE) to de-emphasize Zerubbabel and transfer royal prerogatives to an emerging hierocracy. The final stage (reflected in Zech. 3:8) de-emphasizes the priesthood and refocuses expectation on a future Davidic King (the "Branch").

Martin Hallaschka (2011:303–9, cf. Hallaschka 2012) argues for a similar redaction sequence, but over a longer timeframe. The lampstand vision dates to around 500 BCE, but the Zerubbabel oracles in 4:6-10 were not added until half a century later. The material referring to Joshua (3:1-10 and 6:9-15) was not added until the end of the Persian period at the earliest, because it was only in this era that the High Priest could have such an elevated political position.

Heinz-Gunther Schöttler, in contrast, inverts the sequence of redaction. In his view, Joshua was introduced in the first revision of the visions, which occurred soon after the completion of the temple. This revision centered the visions on the temple cultus and the role of the High Priest. It was not until the mid-fifth century BCE that Zech. 4:6-10 was inserted, to characterize Zerubbabel as the temple builder (Schöttler 1987:291–301).

Lena-Sofia Tiemeyer also argues for a three-stage redaction of Zechariah 3 and 4, but on a timeline that has these chapters being the product of the late sixth century BCE. The primary visionary experience (and its early oracular interpretation) occurred prior to 520 BCE, the oracles relating to the temple occurred around 520 BCE, followed by a post-Zerubbabel redaction. Tiemeyer argues—convincingly in my view—that "it is reasonable to view the material in Zech. 3 and 4, both the visionary material and the oracular material, to stem from the 6th century b.c.e., i.e., from a time when the historical characters of Joshua and Zerubbabel were still alive and when the temple needed to be rebuilt and its governance organized and structured" (2019:75).

4.4.4 Are Zechariah 1:1-6 and Zechariah 7–8 Part of an "Editorial Framework"?

There are clear thematic connections between Zech. 1:1-6 and Zechariah 7–8. These two units of material act as a frame around the night visions. Ackroyd (1952:155) theorized that these two units had been added to the book to provide an editorial framework for the vision and oracles of Zechariah in order to adapt their message to a later generation, and that this editing was part of a larger project that involved adding a similar framework to the book of Haggai.

Similarly, Beuken argued that the editorial framework was added in a chronistic milieu to transform a series of prophetic oracles into a chronicle (1967:331–6). Beuken's argument was based on ideology and phraseology in Zechariah 1–8, which he identified as distinctively "Chronistic." However, the nature and extent of these parallels have since been called into question (see §3.4).

The trend in more recent scholarship has been to date the editorial framework much closer in time to the ministry of the prophet Zechariah. For example, Meyers and Meyers (1987:xlv) argue that the editorial framework was added to Haggai and Zechariah 1–8 in order to create a single composite work some time prior to the rededication of the temple in 515 BCE.

4.5 Genre—The Form of Zechariah's Night Visions

Most of Zechariah's visions conform to the pattern of a vision report (Behrens 2002; Stead 2012).

- The vision report begins "I lifted up my eyes and saw."
- The vision begins with a "surprise clause"—"Behold!"
- The objects in the visions are symbolic (i.e., they represent something else).
- The meaning of the vision is revealed via dialogue.

The form of these visions is a hybrid from multiple sources. The majority of the night visions follow the formal pattern of Jacob's vision in Gen. 31:10-12. However, Genesis 31 only explains some elements of the form of Zechariah's visions. Two of the visions in Zechariah 4 and 5 use the same "what do you see?" dialogue pattern utilized in Amos and Jeremiah. Furthermore, Zechariah's "angelic interpreter" would appear to be a development of the man in Ezekiel's vision who interprets the meaning of the visions (see, e.g., Ezek. 47:1-12). Niditch argues that Zechariah's night visions are a development of the classical symbolic vision as exemplified in Amos and Jeremiah, exhibiting an increasing mythologization of symbol objects and symbolism (1983:74).

The form of the "Joshua" vision in Zechariah 3 is different from the other night visions. Rather than drawing on the form of Genesis 31/Amos/Jeremiah, this vision bears striking similarities to "divine council scenes," especially Isaiah 6. Both passages denote that which is seen by the prophet using a direct object marker with a participial construction instead of a "surprise clause"; both passages omit the expected "I lifted my eyes and looked"; in both passages the prophet becomes a participant in the scene (Isa. 6:8; Zech. 3:5), and both passages describe a cleansing from sin of an identified historical person. The Joshua vision in Zechariah 3 has a different form—*not* because it is a clumsy addition by a later redactor—but because it (like Isaiah 6) is not merely a *symbolic vision*, but also a *symbolic act* that involves the prophet. The difference in function is marked by a difference in form. On this analysis, there is no compelling reason to excise Zechariah 3 from the original "night vision" unit. Rather, the sequence of eight visions should be read as a cohesive unit.

4.6 Zechariah's Visions and the Emergence of Apocalyptic

As we shall discuss in more detail in §5.7, apocalyptic is defined as "a genre of revelatory literature with a narrative framework in which a revelation is mediated by an otherworldly being to a human recipient, disclosing a transcendent reality which is both temporal, insofar as it envisages eschatological salvation, and spatial, insofar as it involves another, supernatural world" (Collins 1979:9).

The visions in Zechariah 1–6 exhibit many of the formal features of apocalyptic—visions of the heavenly realm, an interpreting angel, other heavenly figures, animal symbolism, number symbolism, other highly symbolic imagery, etc.

As a result of this, some scholars connect Zechariah 1–8 with the emergence of "apocalyptic," regarding it as a "proto-apocalyptic" work, in which the disappointments of the early postexilic period resulted in a shift away from the expectation of an historical fulfillment and toward an eschatological one (e.g., Amsler 1972, Gese 1973, cf. Cook 1995).

However, apocalyptic eschatology looks not for Yahweh's intervention *in history*, but for Yahweh's intervention to *end history*, because the present evil age has become so corrupt that Yahweh must bring this age to an end and begin again with a new creation. In contrast, Zechariah 1–8 anticipates Yahweh's action in connection with the historical events of the early postexilic period and therefore does not have an apocalyptic eschatology (North 1972; Jeremias 1977:227). Hanson argues that any apparent similarities to apocalyptic were only because "[t]he genre of the vision was used by Zechariah as a literary device in a campaign to win popular support for the hierocratic temple program" (1979:258). Collins finds that the eschatology of Zechariah 1–8 is not apocalyptic "in any plausible sense of the word" (2003:82). Instead, he argues that Zechariah anticipated the imminent fulfillment—in history—of the prophetic hopes, particularly the promise of a messiah.

We shall return to the question of the emergence of apocalyptic as a type of literature in the next chapter (§5.7) in relation to Zechariah 9–14.

4.7 Intertextuality—Zechariah and the "Former Prophets"

The reference to the "former prophets" in Zech. 1:4 is an early indication of the significance of the reuse of the prophetic tradition in Zechariah 1–8. A number of scholars have examined the extent of continuity of the message of Zechariah 1–8 with the classical prophetic tradition, especially Petitjean (1969), Jeremias (1977), Tollington (1993), Nurmela (1996), and Delkurt (2000). See §5.4 for a discussion of the implication of different methodological approaches to intertextuality.

In my analysis of the intertextuality of Zechariah 1–8 (Stead 2009), I identify three distinctive features.

1. Textual mosaic—it is a highly allusive text, made up of a mosaic of other texts.
2. Sustained allusion—there are repeated references to "background" passages, which stretch across multiple passages.
3. Composite metaphors—the simultaneous allusion to imagery from multiple source passages, which weave hitherto distinct traditions together.

In the overview of Zechariah 1–8 in §4.9, significant intertexts are highlighted with *[]*. For further analysis, see Stead (2009).

4.8 Structure

The three date formulas in Zech. 1:1, 1:7, and 7:1 function as structural markers that divide the material into three units.

I.   The call to return (1:1-6)
II. The night visions and oracles (1:7–6:15)
III. The question from Bethel (Zech. 7:1–8:23)

The central (and largest) unit in Zech. 1:7–6:15 consists of a sequence of eight "night visions" (as they are commonly known) together with associated oracles. The eight visions are concentric, both starting and ending with visions of horses going throughout the earth. There are clear (antithetical) parallels between the first three visions and the last three. In the first three visions, the cumulative picture is of the return of Yahweh and his people to Jerusalem, gathered around his "house." This movement toward Jerusalem is paralleled by an inverse movement in the final three visions, which describe those who are "going out" (Zech. 5:3, 5:6, 6:1)—that is, a movement away from Jerusalem, in which sin and iniquity are purged from the land and relocated to Babylon to a "house" to be built for it there. This is represented diagrammatically in Figure 4.2.

The first three visions and the last three visions form a frame around the two core visions (4 and 5). The core visions—about Joshua the temple-priest in Zechariah 3 (vision 4) and Zerubbabel the temple-builder in Zechariah 4 (vision 5)—describe the means by which sin will be dealt with and by which Yahweh will return to dwell with his people. The structure of the night visions signals the centrality of the temple and its cultus in the Lord's plans to return to dwell with his people.

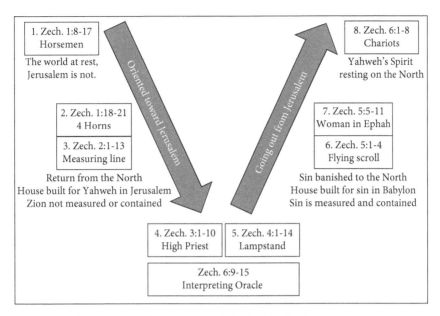

Figure 4.2 The concentric structure of Zech. 1:8–6:15

Zechariah 7–8 are a unified section with a balanced chiastic (A—B—B'—A') structure.

7:2   People from Bethel come to Jerusalem to entreat Yahweh
  7:3-6   Fasting
    7:7–8:17   Zechariah's sermon(s)
  8:18-19   Fasts will turn into feasts
8:20-22   Nations and cities come to Jerusalem to entreat Yahweh

4.9 Overview of Zechariah 1–8—Key Issues

Key intertexts are marked with []—see §2.5 and §4.7.

[I] The Call to Return (Zechariah 1:1-6)

The book of Zechariah begins by authenticating Zechariah as the prophet of Yahweh, providing a summary of his message, and giving a narrative account of the response of his first hearers. The essence of his message is a call to repentance and a promise—"Return to me and I will return to you" *[cf. Joel 2:12-14]*.

The oracle commences with the declaration "Yahweh was very angry with your fathers," alluding to the outworking of that anger, which had resulted in the destruction of Jerusalem in 586 BCE and the exile in Babylon *[Isa. 54:8]*. Zechariah's exhortation to his generation is based on words spoken by the "former prophets" to a former generation.

Zechariah's hearers are told not to be like their fathers, to whom the prophets had preached "turn from your evil ways and your evil practices" *[Jer. 25:5, 7]*, but who had refused to listen and were "overtaken" by the (curses of) the "words and statues" of God's law *[Deut. 28:15]*.

Zechariah 1:5 poses the rhetorical question: "And the prophets—do they live forever?" With Beuken (1967:100) and Rudolph (1976:69) I take this to be referring to false prophets, who suffered the same fate as the fathers. The alternative view is that this clause is setting up an implied contrast with the next verse—"prophets don't live forever, but the word of Yahweh spoken through them endures forever" (e.g., Petersen 1984:133–4).

Scholars are divided as to whether Zech. 1:6b ("they repented") records the repentance of "the fathers" (e.g., Floyd 2000:322) or to the repentance of Zechariah's hearers (e.g., Boda 2004:176). The consensus view is the latter—if the fathers had repented, then why would Zechariah tell his generation "do not be like your fathers"?

The repentance of Zechariah's generation includes an acknowledgment that Yahweh's judgment was what he had purposed to do *[Lam. 2:17]*. Their repentance satisfies the precondition ("Return to me") of Yahweh's promise "I will return to you." As such, the rhetorical effect of Zech. 1:6 is to create the expectation that what follows will, to some degree, describe Yahweh's return, which involves both a relational return ("I will return with mercy"—Zech. 1:16) and a spatial return ("I will return to Zion and dwell in Jerusalem"—Zech. 8:3).

In Zech. 1:1-6, the repentance of the people is described primarily in moral terms (i.e., turning from evil ways and deeds). However, the canonical placement and chronological framework that links Haggai with Zechariah 1–8 adds another dimension. Zechariah 1:1-6 is dated just prior to the laying of the foundation of the temple and, along with the preaching of Haggai, this message led to the refounding of the temple (Zech. 8:9, cf. Ezra 5:1-2). The people's repentance was also manifest in a commitment to temple reconstruction.

The repentance of the people is presupposed by the night visions that follow in Zech. 1:7–6:15, in that there is no further call for repentance in these chapters (in part contra Wenzel 2011).

[II] The Night Visions and Oracles (Zechariah 1:7–6:15)

On the twenty-fourth day of the eleventh month—exactly two months after the refounding of the temple—the prophet Zechariah has a vision "in the night" (1:8). The "night vision" sequence is to be read as occurring during one evening (regardless of whether the oracles were added later).

Zechariah 1:8-17—First Vision

Zechariah's first vision is of a man on a red horse surrounded by other colored horses amid the "myrtles in the deep." Beyond the fact that the colored horses are a point of connection with the eighth vision, the vision attaches no significance to the color of the horses. Similarly, there is no significance attached to the myrtle trees except that they function as a consistent point of reference, which identifies the man on the red horse as the "angel of Yahweh," in that each is described as standing among the myrtles.

The colored horses are sent by Yahweh to go back and forth in the world, and to report back to Yahweh *[cf. Job 1:7, 2:22]*. The horses represent heavenly beings sent on a reconnaissance mission. Their mission is unusual, in that elsewhere horses in Yahweh's service are sent out for battle *[Hab. 3:8, Joel 2:4-5, Isa. 66:15, and Zech. 6:1-8]*. These heavenly scouts report back to the Angel of Yahweh that the whole world is at rest and in peace *[cf. Ezek. 38:11-12]*.

By the second year of Darius, the political tumult of recent years in the Persian Empire had largely subsided (see §1.5; for a counter view, see Wolters 2008). However, a world at rest and in peace is contrary to the expectation raised by the former prophets, who promised that it would be Yahweh's people—not the nations—who enjoyed peace and security (see Jer. 30:10-11, Jer. 46:27-28, and Isa. 32:18), and the nations would be been overthrown. For example, *[Jer. 25:12]* promises that, after "seventy years," Babylon will be punished and made desolate forever.

In response to the report received from the heavenly scouts, the Angel of Yahweh responds in lament form ("How long O Yahweh … " *[Isa. 6:11; Ps.*

80:5] at Yahweh's ongoing anger "these seventy years" (1:12). Zechariah 1:12 picks up the motif of seventy years from Jeremiah 25 and 29, but with a twist. Whereas Jer. 25:9-11 describes the seventy years of Babylon's supremacy (perhaps commencing 605 BCE when Nebuchadnezzar became the king of Babylon), the seventy years in Zech. 1:12 refer to the period of Jerusalem's desolation, commencing in 586 BCE. Zechariah's innovation is to see these two periods of seventy years as not coterminus. The rhetorical effect of the mention of seventy years has the opposite effect to that which it had in the book of Jeremiah. In Jeremiah, "seventy years" meant a long wait, whereas for Zechariah's generation, at the cusp of the end of the seventy years, the reuse of this motif raises the hope of an imminent reversal of fortunes.

In response to the lament in v. 12, Yahweh speaks "good words" (cf. Jer. 29:10-11, 33:14) and "comforting words" *[Isa. 40:1-8]* to the interpreting angel (who is not to be confused with the Angel of Yahweh). What is spoken to the interpreting angel in Zech. 1:13 is presumably what the angel commands Zechariah to proclaim in 1:14-17—a message of restoration and "comfort" (1:17).

Zechariah 1:14-15 announces that a reversal of fortunes has already taken place. Whereas in the past Yahweh was "very angry" with the fathers (1:2), now he is "very angry" at the nations, and "very jealous" for his people *[Isa. 54:7-8]*. Yahweh holds the nations accountable for how they treated his people, notwithstanding that they were instruments of his judgment. Zechariah 1:15 picks up Isaiah's words against specific nations like Assyria *[Isa. 10:5-15]* and Babylon *[Isa. 47:6, 54:7ff]*, and applies them against all nations who in their arrogance "feel secure" (like Assyria) and have "added to the calamity" (like Babylon) by their exploitation of God's people when given into their hands.

Zechariah 1:16-17 is the flipside of the reversal of fortunes for the nations—a message of restoration, rebuilding, and renewal for the people of God. These verses combine the promises of *[Isa. 52:8-9]* (Yahweh's return to Zion) and *[Isa. 54:7]* ("in mercy") with the promise in *[Isa. 44:26-28]* that the temple would be rebuilt after the exile.

The restoration of Jerusalem is depicted via two motifs—a "measuring line" and "overflowing towns." Elsewhere, a measuring line stretched out over Jerusalem is an image of destruction *[Lam. 2:8]*. But here, consistent with the "reversal" theme, this negative image has been inverted. The measuring line will now be used—not for destruction—but for construction, like the measuring line described in *[Jer. 31:38-39]* used to rebuild the walls of

Jerusalem. The motif of "overflowing towns" depicts the abundance of God's blessing *[e.g., Isa. 54:2-3]*. This motif is further developed in Zech. 2:4.

The final verse reiterates the message of reversal—"Yahweh will *again comfort Zion* and *again choose Jerusalem*." As noted above, the promise of comfort for Zion activates the promises of Isaiah 40–55 (e.g., *[Isa. 51:3]*). Yahweh "chooses" a place in order to "put his name there for his dwelling" *[Deut. 12:5]*, here indicating Yahweh's intention to again return to dwell in the midst of his people.

Zechariah 1:18-21 [MT 2:1-4]—Second Vision

In the second vision, Zechariah first sees four horns, which represent "the horns of the nations" (1:21 [MT 2:4]). The horn is often used in the Old Testament as a metaphor for strength. These four horns therefore symbolize mighty nations, which have "scattered Judah, Israel and Jerusalem" (1:19 [MT 2:2], cf. *[Jer. 50:17-18, Joel 3:2 (MT 4:2)]*).

Elsewhere in Zechariah, the number four is used to symbolize universality (e.g., four winds of heaven [2:6 [MT 2:10], 6:5], four chariots [6:1]). Likewise, in this vision the four horns represent any and all nations who seek to scatter God's people.

Zechariah then sees four "craftsmen" (or "blacksmiths"). These four are "craftsmen of destruction" *[Ezek. 21:31 (MT 21:36)]*, who are Yahweh's instruments of judgment on the nations who have "lifted up their horns" to scatter Judah, humiliating them so that "no head could be raised." That situation will be reversed when the craftsmen "terrify" and "cast down" the horns of the nations (1:21 [MT 2:4]).

Zechariah 2:1-13 [MT 2:5-17]—Third Vision

The third vision is of a man with a measuring cord, which combines elements of *[Ezekiel 40]* and *[Jer. 31:38-39]*. Like Ezekiel 40, this man uses a measuring cord (40:3) and measures "width" and "breadth" (40:7). But like Jeremiah 31—and unlike Ezekiel 40—this man is measuring Jerusalem, presumably with a view to rebuilding the walls (cf. Jer. 31:38-39).

The message of this vision is that the walls should not be rebuilt— Jerusalem will be a city without walls *[Ezek. 38:11]*, because Yahweh is going to repopulate the city with an overflowing abundance of people and their livestock.

The vulnerability of a city without walls is addressed by the promise that Yahweh will be a wall of fire around it, reversing the imagery of *[Lam. 2:3]*. Moreover, Yahweh also promises, "I will be the glory in her midst," which anticipates the return of God's glorious presence to the temple *[Ezek. 43:1-5, 43:7]*.

As noted in §4.4 above, some interpretations of Zechariah 2 seek to separate the two oracles in 2:6-9 [MT 2:10-13] and 2:10-13 [MT 2:13-17] from the vision (and embedded oracle) in 2:1-5 [MT 2:5-9] on the basis that the oracle about fleeing from Babylon in 2:6-9 [MT 2:10-13] interrupts the sequence between the promise of Yahweh's "glory in her midst" in 2:5 [MT 2:9] and the oracle about Yahweh "dwelling in the midst" in 2:10-13 [MT 2:13-17]. However, the current arrangement is readily explicable. Zech. 2:1-5 [MT 2:5-9] contains two promises—the repopulation of Jerusalem and the return of the glory of Yahweh, and the two oracles that follow address each promise in turn.

While it is true that the first oracle reflects a broad prophetic tradition of anti-Babylon oracles (Boda 2008), what is distinctive about this oracle is that those who "flee" and "escape" from Babylon *[Jer. 51:6]* are called upon to flee *to Zion*. The oracle is addressed to those whom Yahweh has "scattered," and the rhetorical intent is to bring about their return from exile in Babylon in order to address the first promise in the vision (i.e., a repopulated Jerusalem). The prophet is sent to the nations "after glory" (i.e., "for the sake of Yahweh's honour"—see *[Ezek. 39:21]*, Tiemeyer 2004, Stead 2009:121–3).

The second oracle celebrates the impending return of Yahweh to dwell in the midst of his people, drawing together elements from *[Isa. 12:6/Zeph. 3:14-15/ Joel 2:23, 27, Ezek. 37:26-27, and 43:1-9]*. Remarkably, this promise extends to people from "many nations" *[Isa. 2:3]* who will be "joined to Yahweh" in that day *[Isa. 14:1, 56:3]*. Even more remarkably, the covenant formula—"they will be my people"—is applied outside the covenant people of God.

Zechariah 2:10-13 is temple-centric, reflected in the promise to "dwell in the midst" *[Ezek. 37:26-28]*, "holy ground" *[Exod. 3:5]*, the "choice of Jerusalem" (see comments above on 1:17), and the allusion to *[Hab. 2:20]* in the final verse.

Zechariah 3:1-10—Fourth Vision

As noted above (§4.5), the form of Zechariah 3 differs from the other night visions, reflecting the fact that this symbolic vision also involves a symbolic act. It contains an amalgam of imagery from *[Isa. 6]* and *[Job 1-2]*. In the vision, the High Priest Joshua is symbolically "snatched from the fire" *[Amos*

4:11], cleansed from sin and reclothed in the garments of the High Priest. As Boda (2017:63) notes, "the consistent use of vocabulary from priestly rituals strongly suggests that the scene reflects the investiture and atonement rituals of the high priest."

Scholars differ as to whether Joshua is given four commands (walk in my ways; keep my charge; administer justice; keep my courts), and a single promise, of access in the heavenly court (e.g., Redditt 1995:64–5) whether he is given two commands and three promises (e.g., Floyd 2000:372).

Scholars also differ as to whether Zechariah 3 represents a *restoration* of the proper functions of the priesthood (e.g., Stead 2009:161–4) or an *elevation* of the role of the priesthood at the expense of the role of the monarchy (e.g., Meyers and Meyers 1987:195–7), and if the latter, as to whether this reflects the context of the sixth century BCE or a subsequent century.

Different scholarly views about these matters lead to markedly different conclusions about the meaning of the oracle in vv. 3:8-10. Most scholars agree (but contra Petersen 1984:209) that this oracle addressed to Joshua and "his associates" applies to the priesthood as a whole, and through them for all the people. But there is little agreement about the connection (if any) between the priesthood being a "sign" and Yahweh's promise "I am going to bring my servant the Branch" in v. 9. For example, Tiemeyer (2006:240) removes Zech. 3:8b as a secondary insertion, so that the "sign" of the priesthood in Zech. 3:8a instead points to the removal of sin (on the Day of Atonement) in Zech. 3:9. Petersen (1984:214) argues that the "Branch" is a later addition of the chapter to restore an emphasis on the Davidic monarchy.

There is general agreement that the title "Branch" alludes to **[Jer. 23:5-6]** (and cf. Jer. 33:14-18). In the Jeremian context, the use of the title "Branch" looks forward to the restoration of a righteous Davidic line after the exile. This was necessary because of the desolation of the house of David due to a succession of unrighteous Davidic kings (see esp. Jer. 22:5, 11, 18, 24, and 30).

My own view (which I acknowledge is a minority position) argues the restoration of the priesthood is a sign *that* Yahweh will bring "my servant the Branch." The logic of this sign requires that a reader recognizes that the "Branch," because he is a royal son of David, is also a temple-builder (2 Sam. 7:12-13, cf. Zech. 6:12), and therefore the restoration of the priesthood—which cannot operate without a temple—necessarily implies that Yahweh will raise up a temple builder (and the only appropriate person to build the temple is a royal son of David). This interpretation depends on reading Zech. 3:9 in the light of Zech. 4:9 and Zech. 6:12. Since Zerubbabel will build the temple (4:9), and the "Branch" will build the temple (6:12), therefore

Zerubbabel is the Branch. This assumes that the temple being referred to throughout is the one in which Joshua and his associates will exercise their ministry.

Another interpretation, which has been common since Wellhausen, is that while Zechariah 1–8 originally identified Zerubbabel as the messianic branch, this has been subsequently redacted out because of the failure of Zerubbabel to live up to messianic expectations. In particular, Zechariah 6 has recast these expectations in terms of an anonymous future figure and (perhaps) a spiritual, rather than physical, temple (see, e.g., Mason 1982:148).

An alternative interpretation is that the title "Branch" never referred to Zerubbabel and instead was addressed at the outset to a future figure, who will build a future temple (e.g., Rose 2000:248–9).

Continuing the promise of Zech. 3:8, Zech. 3:9 describes a "single stone with seven eyes," which Yahweh has set before Joshua, and upon which Yahweh will "engrave its inscription," which is associated with the removal of iniquity of the land in a single day.

There are no shortages of possible interpretations of this "single stone with seven eyes," whether in isolation, or in conjunction with the various stones and "seven lamps/eyes" in Zechariah 4. However, as VanderKam (1991:562) notes, two views on the "stone" in Zechariah 3 have come to dominate—either that the stone is part of Joshua's High-Priestly vestments, or that the stone is for the construction of the temple. Taking the view that it is the former, this stone is best understood as an amalgam of two objects in Exodus 28—the "engraved plate" of the holy crown *[Exod. 28:36]* and the two stones engraved with the names of the twelve tribes *[Exod. 28:11-12]*. This is part of the recommissioning of Joshua to represent the people before Yahweh on the Day of Atonement, when sin is removed "in a single day" (see also Pola 2003:222; Tiemeyer 2006:249). This will usher in the paradisiacal peace described in Zech. 3:10 *[cf. Mic. 4:4]*.

Zechariah 4:1-14–Fifth Vision

Zechariah 4 contains a vision of a lampstand, drawing on the imagery of the tabernacle lampstand *[esp. Exod. 25:31-39; 27:20]*, and two oracles, one *to* Zerubbabel and one *about* Zerubbabel.

A key interpretive issue for Zech. 4:1-14 is the extent to which the two Zerubbabel oracles in Zech. 4:6b-10aβ relate to the vision of the lampstand in 4:1-6a and the interpretation of that vision in 4:10b-14. Verses 4:6b-10aβ are clearly disjunctive with their context, because they interrupt the vision and its interpretation. However, taking scissors to the text does not satisfactorily resolve the problem. Indeed, as van der Woude (1988:238–9) has demonstrated, this approach creates more problems than it solves. Moreover, these oracles must be nearly contemporaneously with the visions, since they postdate the founding of the temple and predate its completion (Niditch 1983:94, Tiemeyer 2019). Figure 4.3 shows the correspondence between vision and interpretation.

The oracles begin with an assurance to Zerubbabel that he will complete the temple "not by might, nor by power" *[Ps. 33:16]* "but by my Spirit" *[Hag. 2:5]*. Yahweh will turn the mountains into a level plain *[Isa. 40:4]*, whether they be "mountains of rubble" (Tollington 1993:148–9) or "mountains of trouble" (Floyd 2000:381).

There is much debate about the significance of the stones in these oracles. Is the stone in 4:7 a "first stone" (=foundation; Meyers and Meyers 1987: 246–9) or "head stone" (=capstone; Mason 1977:55)? Similarly, is the stone in 4:9 a "tin stone" (=plumb bob, used in construction; Mitchell 1912:191) or a "set-apart stone" (=the final stone for the new temple; Edelman 2005:125)? However, whatever the particular role of these two stones in the construction process, the overall message of both oracles is clear from v. 9: the hands of Zerubbabel have laid the foundation, and the hands of Zerubbabel will complete the temple.

If the Zerubbabel oracles have been intentionally inserted (either in a literary sense or redactional sense—see Meyers and Meyers 1987:242, 65–72) in order to clarify the meaning of the lampstand, then it is reasonable to conclude that the lampstand symbolizes a functioning temple (Rost 1951:220), because

Figure 4.3 Vision and interpretation in Zechariah 4

Vision (Zech. 4:2-3)	Interpretation (Zech. 4:6-14)
A lampstand, all of gold, and a bowl upon the top of it.	*[either unexplained or explained by 4:6-10aβ]* The hands of Zerubbabel laid the foundation of this house; his hands shall also complete it (Zech. 4:9).
seven lamps on it—seven, and seven pipes for the lamps, which are on the top of it.	These seven are the eyes of Yahweh, which range through the whole earth (Zech. 4:10b).
And by it there are two olive trees, one on the right of the bowl and the other on its left.	What are these two branches of the olive trees, which pour out the oil through the two golden pipes? … "These are the two sons of oil who stand before the Lord of the whole earth" (Zech. 4:12-14).

the oracles declare that Zerubbabel will complete the temple, and the vision of a blazing lampstand depicts the same reality—a completed, operative temple.

If, on the other hand, the purpose of the Zerubbabel oracles is not to give the interpretation of the lampstand, then there are other options—either that the lampstand symbolizes Yahweh, because of the apparent connection with his "eyes" in 4:10 (e.g., Petersen 1984:234), or that it symbolizes the worshipping community (e.g., Baldwin 1972:124).

The other key elements in the vision are the "seven lamps" and the "two sons of oil" (taking the "bowl" and the "7 spouts (?)" and "two pipes" to be incidental details, for which no interpretation is given).

On the view taken here that the lampstand represents the temple, the "seven lamps" represent Yahweh's presence in the temple. Light and fire are common symbols of God's presence with his people. The light shining forth from the seven lamps symbolizes the "seven eyes" (the all-seeing presence) of Yahweh (4:10).

There is some debate about the identity and function of the two olive trees, which signify the "two sons of oil who stand before the Lord." Most commentators identify these two figures as Joshua and Zerubbabel (contra Boda 2004:275, who argues for Haggai and Zechariah), with many taking the view that this vision depicts some form of political diarchy between the two.

However, the oil, which flows from the two olive trees, and which is integral to the vision, is irrelevant to this interpretation. We should instead begin with the question—how do the two olive trees provide oil to the lampstand?—or in non-symbolic terms—how do Zerubbabel and Joshua enable the functioning of the temple? They each do this in different ways. Zerubbabel "provides oil" to the temple through his role in building it, and Joshua "provides oil" through his role as High Priest in the temple (Stead 2009:181–5).

Zechariah 5:1-4—Sixth Vision

There is a broad consensus that the sixth vision depicts the land being cleansed of immorality. Yahweh purges sin by means of a curse-bearing scroll *[Deut. 29:20; Jer. 36:3; Ezek. 2:10]*. The two sins identified echo two of the Ten Commandments (you shall not steal; you shall not bear false witness), but using a form of words from *[Jer. 7:9-10]*. The flying scroll in Zech. 5:1-4 is a vivid representation of the curses of the covenant.

Scholars interpret the details differently—for example, whether there is significance to the size of the scroll (Meyers and Meyers 1987:280–3), whether the two sins being purged are representative of (say) the Decalogue as a whole or are addressed to specific issues of theft and false witness in the postexilic community in relation to disputes over the ownership of real estate between the returnees and those who had remained in the land (Redditt 1995:72), and whether the correct translation of the Hebrew verb *niqqâ* in v. 3 is "to purge" sin or "to acquit" sin, and so whether this clause describes the enactment of God's judgment to purge sinners (so most scholars), or the reason for God's judgment in v. 4, because human courts have acquitted the guilty party (Petterson 2014).

Zechariah 5:5-11—Seventh Vision

Zechariah 5:5-11 describes a vision of a woman (identified as "wickedness") confined in an ephah basket. The ephah is borne by stork-winged women toward Shinar (i.e., Babylon) where a "house" is to be built for it.

The seventh vision does not have an associated interpretive oracle, which has led to a plethora of possible interpretations (see, e.g., Love 1999:205–14; Edelman 2003.

Some interpretations focus on the ephah, connecting this with the "dishonest ephah" motif (e.g., Deut. 24:14-15, Amos 8:5, Mic. 6:10). However, the measuring function of the ephah is not highlighted in this vision.

Most interpretations center on the woman rather than the ephah basket. While some understand the woman simply as a feminine-personified metaphor for sin (e.g., Eve, Jerusalem, the prostitute, menstrual uncleanness), the better approach is to see that the woman in ephah represents a particular form of wickedness—idolatry—on the basis that "the wickedness" (*hāriš'â*) is a near anagram for "the Asherah" (*hā'ăšērâ*, cf. 2 Kgs 21:7), and that the vision therefore depicts the removal of idolatry from the land. On the basis of intertextual connections with *[Ezekiel 1-11]*, I argue that Zech. 5:5-11 depicts an "anti-ark" borne by "anti-cherubs," to be put in an "anti-temple" in an "anti-Jerusalem" (Stead 2009:197).

Zechariah 6:1-8—Eighth Vision

The colored horses in the final vision link to the horses in the first vision, but with an important difference. Whereas the horses in the first vision go out on a recognizance mission only, these horses go out with war chariots *[cf. Hab. 3:8, Joel 2:4-5]* from standing in the presence of Yahweh *[Job 1:6-7]*.

There are two exegetical decisions that impact the interpretation of the final vision.

The first is the direction taken by the white horses. Literally, they go "to the rear of them," but does this mean "behind the back horses"—that is, also to the North (so Floyd 2000:400), or they go "rearwards"—that is, West (so Rudolph 1976:123, Mitchell 1912:180).

The second issue is whether Yahweh's Spirit being "set at rest" in the land of the North (i.e., Babylon) is positive, in that it signifies that Yahweh's rule has been established there (e.g., Niditch 1983:156), or negative, in that it signifies that Yahweh's anger has been given rest because the war chariots have executed judgment on the Land of the North (e.g., Jeremias 1977:27). The textual echoes of *[Ezek. 13:13 and 24:13]* in this verse help to resolve that the latter interpretation is preferable. This interpretation also provides a resolution to the issue left hanging at the end of the seventh vision— Yahweh has not relocated the worship of Asherah to Babylon so that it might thrive there, but so that it would be destroyed along with Babylon.

Zechariah 6:9-15

Zechariah 6:9-15 describes a symbolic act involving a crown or crowns. There is some debate as to whether there are one or two crowns. There are two references to crown(s) in this section—one in v. 11 and the other in v. 14. The first is a plural form ("crowns") and the second is a different form that could either be plural or singular, but in context should be read as a singular, because it is followed by a singular verb (Meyers and Meyers 1987:349–53, 362–3).

Some explain the discrepancy in crowns as arising from a clumsy redaction, arguing that the text originally had referred to the crowning of Zerubbabel, but that the failure of messianic expectations surrounding Zerubbabel led to a revision of the passage to focus on Joshua instead (e.g., Redditt 1995:256).

However, the text can be read coherently as is. Reading plural "crowns" in v. 11 and a singular "crown" in v. 14, Zechariah is being told to take gold and silver and have crowns made, and to put one of the crowns on the head of Joshua the High Priest (6:11). Zechariah is to proclaim a message to Joshua about someone else called "the Branch" (6:12-13) and is told to perform a second symbolic act with the other crown (6:14).

The significance of this "Branch" comes from key intertexts from Jeremiah (23:5, 22:30, 33:16-18) and 2 Samuel 7 (Stead 2009:137–53). Yahweh will raise up a Davidic "Branch" *[Jer. 23:5]* to restore what Jehoiachin lost—a son of David to "sit and rule on his throne" *[Jer. 22:30]*. In the future, the Davidic Branch and the priesthood will operate in tandem *[Jer. 33:16-18]*. Zerubbabel is called "Branch" (though not "*the* Branch") because he is a son of David who will build the temple for Yahweh *[2 Sam. 7:13]*.

This oracle should be read consistent with Zech. 3:8-10 and 4:6-10. Zechariah 3 consists of a symbolic act involving Joshua (3:1-7) accompanied by an oracle to Joshua about an absent but coming "Branch" (3:8). Likewise in Zechariah 6 the symbolic act of Joshua's crowning is accompanied by an oracle to Joshua about a coming "Branch." These should be read in parallel. Similarly, in Zech. 4:10, Zerubbabel is identified as the temple builder, and in 6:12-13 the "Branch" is the temple-builder, therefore Zerubbabel is the Branch.

It is important to recognize that the two crowns have different functions. The first crown is to be "set … on the head of the high priest, Joshua son of Jehozadak" (6:11) and the other will be "as a memorial in the temple of Yahweh" (6:14). Joshua's crown is NOT to signify the transfer of royal power to the priesthood (contra Beuken; see §4.4.3). Rather, it is the completion of his investiture in the garments of a high priest—"the gold plate, the holy crown" on his turban *[cf. Lev. 8:9]*. Joshua's crown is symbolic of his responsibility to govern Yahweh's house and administer his courts (Zech. 3:7).

The fact that the second crown is not given to the "Branch" but instead is put "as a memorial in the temple of Yahweh" indicates that this vision does not anticipate Zerubbabel's "crowning" as king. Thus, even though the intertexts tell us that Zerubbabel is the temple-building branch through whom the Davidic line is reestablished after its cessation in the exile, Zechariah 6 stops short of identifying Zerubbabel as the coming King. That is, this oracle signals that Zerubbabel is only a *partial* fulfillment of the "Branch" prophecies of Jeremiah 23 and Jeremiah 33.

The description of the Branch "on his throne" and a priest "on his throne" with a "counsel of peace between them" does not refer to a political diarchy *per se*, but each exercising authority in their respective "seat" of responsibility. This same reality is depicted in vision form by the two sons of oil in Zech. 4:14.

[III] The Question from Bethel (Zechariah 7:1–8:23)

Zechariah 7:1-2 People from Bethel Come to Jerusalem to Entreat Yahweh

The dating formula locates this sermon to December 518 BCE, close to the midpoint of the temple reconstruction project (see §4.1), and sixty-eight years into the "70 years" of Jerusalem's desolation.

7:3-6 A Question about Fasting

It is at this time the people of Bethel send a delegation led by Sharezer and Regem-Melech to "entreat Yahweh's favour." Typically, one entreats Yahweh's favor that he might relent from judgment *[Jer. 26:19]*. They address their question to the "priests of Yahweh's house and the prophets." Prophets in the plural presumably include Haggai and Zechariah.

The paraphrase of their question in v. 5 provides the hint as to the motivation for their question—they have been fasting "these 70 years." Their various fasts have commemorated the destruction of Jerusalem and its temple. Do they need to continue to fast when the temple reconstruction is well underway, and when they are almost at the end of the "seventy years"?

The proper attitude for a penitential fast is described in *[Joel 2:12]*—"Return to me with all your heart, with fasting and weeping and mourning."

Zechariah's reply in 7:4-6 challenges whether the people have been fasting with the right attitude these past seventy years. Their fasting was more like the hypocritical fast described in *[Isa. 58:3-6]*. The sermon (or sermons) that follows challenge their attitude, by reminding this generation what happened to their fathers in Jeremiah's day, when that generation merely went through the rituals at the temple.

Zechariah 7:7–8:17—Zechariah's Sermon(s)

Although some scholars treat these chapters as containing an anthology of Zechariah's sermons and/or focus on the detection of redactional layers in its composition, they are better read synchronically as a single sermon, with both a retrospective (ch. 7) and prospective (ch. 8) message (Wolters 2014:216–36).

Zechariah 7–8 recapitulates the message of Zechariah 1–6, albeit in a prosaic rather than vision mode (cf. Petersen 1984:123). The close thematic parallels can be seen in Figure 4.4.

Figure 4.4 Parallels between Zechariah 1–6 and 7–8

Yahweh's wrath against the fathers	Rebuilding and return	Implications for Yahweh's people	Implications for the nations
Zech. 1:1-6	Zech. 1:7– 4:14; 6:9-15	Zechariah 5	Zech. 6:1-8
Zech. 7:1-14	Zech. 8:1-15	Zech. 8:16-19	Zech. 8:20-23

The paneling of these two parallel accounts suggests that they are to be read together to get the complete picture. As Boda notes, the addition of Zechariah 7–8 "transcends the agenda of temple rebuilding by accentuating the ethical agenda" (2003:51). Contra Wellhausen (§2.1), Zechariah 7–8 addresses both "cult" and "ethics."

Zechariah 7–8 consists of both intratextual and intertextual allusions. The effect of the intratextual allusions to Zechariah 1–6 is to bind the two sections of Zechariah 1–8 together (see Figure 4.5).

The effect of the intertextual allusions is to add an ethical overlay to Zechariah 1–8 as a whole.

There is a sustained allusion to [Jeremiah 7] in Zech. 7:7-13 (Zech. 7:9-10 || Jer. 7:5-6; Zech. 7:11-12 || Jer. 7:24-25; Zech. 7:12 || 7:20; Zech. 7:13 || Jer. 7:13-16). The rhetorical effect of the allusion to the famous temple sermon in Jeremiah 7 is to warn Zechariah's generation against adopting the "temple = God-in-a-box" mentality of their forebears. The mere completion of the temple will not guarantee the return of Yahweh to dwell with his people. Rather, it must be accompanied by the ethical transformation of the people of God.

In Zechariah 8 there are a string of allusions to "covenant" themes from Deuteronomy, Haggai, and Jeremiah (see Figure 4.6).

Figure 4.5 Intratexts in Zechariah 7–8

Intratextual allusion	Zechariah 7 →	Zech. 1:1-6
the proclamation of a former prophet	Zech. 7:7	Zech. 1:4a
near quotation of Jeremiah	Zech. 7:9-10	Zech. 1:4b
people do not hear or listen	Zech. 7:11-12	Zech. 1:4c
Yahweh's great wrath	Zech. 7:12	Zech. 1:2
consequences for "the fathers"	Zech. 7:13-14	Zech. 1:5-6
	Zechariah 8 →	**Zechariah 1-6**
jealous for Zion with great jealousy	Zech. 8:2	Zech. 1:14
return to Zion and dwell in the midst	Zech. 8:3	Zech. 1:16; 2:10
repopulation of Jerusalem	Zech. 8:4-8	Zech. 2:4-5 [MT 8-9]
hands made strong to build the temple	Zech. 8:9	Zech. 4:6-10
doing good for Jerusalem and Judah	Zech. 8:15	Zech. 1:12,17
false oath	Zech. 8:16-17	Zech. 5:4
many nations joined to Yahweh	Zech. 8:20	Zech. 2:15
God is with you/dwelling in the midst	Zech. 8:23	Zech. 2:15

Figure 4.6 Intertexts in Zechariah 7–8

Intertextual allusion	Zechariah 8→	Deut./Hag./Jer.
covenant blessing/cursing in the nations	Zech. 8:13	Deut. 30:1
enemies going out/coming in	Zech. 8:10	Deut. 28:6-7
no reward for man or beast	Zech. 8:10	Hag. 1:11
earth give its yield; heaven give its dew	Zech. 8:12	Hag. 1:10
before these days	Zech. 8:10	Hag. 2:15
day of the founding of Yahweh's house	Zech. 8:9	Hag. 2:18
let your hands be strong; do not be afraid	Zech. 8:13	Hag. 2:4-5
Jerusalem called faithful & holy mountain	Zech. 8:3	Jer. 31:23
children rejoicing in the streets	Zech. 8:4-5	Jer. 30:19-20; 31:13

Zech. 8:1-17 is a series of seven mini-oracles, each of which begins with the words "This is what Yahweh (of Hosts) says." The intertextual echoes highlight something that is not explicit in Zechariah 1–6: The reason for their imminent reversal of fortunes is not because they are rebuilding the temple; it is because the covenant relationship between God and his people has been restored. Zechariah 8 is a recapitulation of Zechariah 1–6, but told in a way that puts the accent on the restoration of the covenant. The rhetorical effect of these allusions is to make Yahweh's covenant with his people the basis of their ethical response to him (see Stead 2009:245–6).

Zechariah 8:18-19

Zechariah 8:18-19 returns to the question about fasting (cf. 7:3-6). The reason to stop fasting is not because the temple has almost been restored or that the "seventy years" have almost run their course, but because Yahweh has acted to restore his covenant with his people, and the blessings of the covenant are upon them. The right response, therefore, is one of covenant obedience—"love truth and peace."

Zechariah 8:20-23

The picture of future blessing reaches its climax in vv. 20-23. Blessing is not limited to Judah and Jerusalem. Many peoples will entreat the favor of Yahweh. The pilgrimage of the nations to Jerusalem is a development of *[Isa. 2:2-3]*.

5

Zechariah 9–14

5.1 Date

By comparison with Haggai and Zechariah 1–8, where the progression of dating formulas helps to anchor the historical context to the early second temple period, the dating of Zechariah 9–14 is much more complicated. There are no dating formulas, and any allusions to historical events are both sparse and disputed. This has led to proposed dates for Zechariah 9–14 ranging from the eighth to the second centuries BCE.

Wolters (2014:16–23) provides a helpful overview of five broad traditions of scholarship on the dating of Zechariah 9–14 since the mid-sixteenth century, which has been summarized in the following table.

BCE	Scholarly consensus
early fifth	**Zechariah 9–14 was written by the prophet Zechariah**, perhaps some decades after Zechariah 1–8 (which accounts for the differences in style and context). This was the classical interpretation since rabbinic and patristic times, but since the nineteenth century has become a minority position and now held largely only by conservative scholars.
sixth	**Zechariah 9–14 (or parts thereof) was written by Jeremiah**. On the basis of Matt. 27:9, which apparently attributes Zech. 11:13 ("thirty pieces of silver") to Jeremiah, Joseph Mede argued that (at least) Zechariah 9–11 was written by Jeremiah. Scholarly support for this view peaked in the seventeenth and eighteenth centuries.
eighth–sixth	**Zechariah 9–14 is a composite preexilic work by an unknown author**. The references to Israel/Ephraim in Zechariah 9–11 locate these chapters prior to the fall of the Northern Kingdom and are therefore a product of the eighth century BCE. Zechariah 12–14 is later and must postdate the death of Josiah (c. 609 BCE, cf. Zech. 12:11). For most of the nineteenth century, the overwhelming critical consensus supported a preexilic dating of Zechariah 9–14.

BCE	Scholarly consensus
second	**Zechariah 9–14 is dated to the Hellenistic period (i.e., late postexilic).** Stade argued that Zechariah 9-14 was written around 280 BCE. The Hellenistic-era dating quickly became the new consensus of historical criticism and remained so for most of the twentieth century.
fifth	**Zechariah 9–14 was written in the first half of the fifth century** BCE, but (probably) not by the prophet Zechariah, on account of the differences in style and theological outlook to Zechariah 1–8. In recent commentaries, this is emerging as the new "scholarly consensus."

With reference to this history, Wolters comments, "[I]t is perhaps not too much to say that the attempts to date Zechariah [9–14] represents one of the most spectacular failures in the history of biblical scholarship" (2014:16).

Modern scholarship currently divides into two main camps—those who argue for an early Hellenistic date and those who argue for an early to mid-fifth-century date (perhaps within the lifespan of the prophet Zechariah). The first position remains the dominant view in European scholarship, and the second is the dominant view in Anglophone scholarship. To compare the arguments for each position, we will take James Nogalski as representative of the first, and Mark Boda as representative of the second. The question of dating is far from settled, demonstrated by ongoing lively debate (see, e.g., Nogalski's critique of Boda's position in Nogalski 2020:70–4).

Nogalski's argument for an early Hellenistic date follows the trajectory established by Elliger in 1949 in arguing that the north-to-south conquest described in Zech. 9:1-8 reflects the military campaign of Alexander the Great in 332 BCE. Nogalski offers four lines of evidence for a Hellenistic date and against a Persian period date (summarized from Nogalski 2011:809, 2020:71–3).

1. The geographical flow of Zech. 9:1-8 fits well with Alexander's conquest of Syria, Phoenicia, Philistia, and Egypt in 332 BCE.
2. Alexander's defeat of Persia in 333 BCE explains the lack of any explicit reference to Persia in Zechariah 9–14 and also explains why Greece ("the sons of Javan") is the enemy identified in Zech. 9:13. In contrast, had these chapters been written in fifth century BCE, it is hard to account for the absence of any mention of Persia.
3. The social setting presumed in Zechariah 9–14 does not match up particularly well with those in Malachi, Ezra, and Nehemiah—works

that are also frequently (though not universally) dated to the mid- to late fifth century.

4. The literary and intellectual developments of Zechariah 9–14 represent considerable development on several fronts: (1) the proto-apocalyptic outlook, (2) the extensive use of other canonical writings, and (3) the rejection of "Ephraim" in Zechariah 11 make more sense in the aftermath of Alexander, when tensions with Samaria again intensified, than it does in the mid-fifth century.

Boda's argument (2016:34) for a fifth-century date (and against a Hellenistic date) can be summarized as follows.

1. The depiction of the warrior's march in Zech. 9:1-8 does not match Alexander's conquest of the Levant.
2. A late date is not necessary to explain the reference to Greece. The Greeks were a major player in the ancient world from Darius onward.
3. The reference to Egypt is not inconsistent with a fifth-century dating, and the references to Aram and Phoenicia as key geo-political units in Zech. 9:1-8 fit the early Persian period better than they do in a later era.
4. Socio-literary analysis of Zechariah 9–14 (see, e.g., Redditt 1995: 99–100) has linked these texts to the early Persian period.
5. Apocalyptic features are not necessarily an indication of a date in the Hellenistic period.
6. The reference to "weighing out" silver in 11:12 may favor an earlier date, since coinage increasingly dominated mercantile trade after 400 BCE.

While recognizing that the alternative view has much to commend it, this study guide will proceed on the (tentative) basis that Zechariah is a Persian period text. This is based on the following textual clues and inferences.

1. Taking the reference to "my house" in Zech. 9:8 to be a reference to the temple, Yahweh's promise in that verse that oppressors will not "*again overrun them*" indicates that Zechariah 9 postdates the destruction of the temple in 586 BCE. Furthermore, since Zech. 11:13 implies an operative temple, Zechariah 9–11 must postdate 515 BCE.
2. The negative assessment of Israel's leadership in Zechariah 10–11 contrasts sharply with the positive assessment of the High Priest (Joshua) and governor (Zerubbabel) in Zechariah 1–8. Zechariah 10–11 is more congruent with the first half of the fifth century BCE, in an

era when the governors (Neh. 5:15) and priests (Mal. 1:6-2:9) receive adverse assessment.

3. The absence of Persia as a foe in Zechariah 9–14 does not count against this being a Persian-era text. Rather, this is consistent with other Persian-era texts (and beyond) that consistently portray Persia as beneficial (or at least benign) toward Judah. The identification of Greece as a foe (as in Zech. 9:13) becomes increasing more likely after 490 BCE, when Greece soundly defeated Persia at the battle of Marathon (on the basis that the foe of my friend is my foe).

4. While accepting Nogalski's (and Elliger's) argument that Alexander's campaigns are a better historical match for the sequence in Zech. 9:1-8 than other known military incursions in the Levant, this argument assumes that Zech. 9:1-8 must be alluding to a historical conquest. This assumption is not warranted by the text. Rather, Zech. 9:1-8 is a promise that Yahweh the divine warrior will act at an undetermined point in the future against certain places for the sake of his house and his people. To connect this action with the military campaigns of Alexander the Great undermines the rhetorical purposes of the section.

5.2 Text

The MT of Zechariah 9–14 is relatively unproblematic, with minor *ketiv*/*qere* on three verses (Zech. 11:2, 14:2, and 14:6).

Hebrew fragments of Zechariah 9–14 are found in 4QXII^g (10:11-12:3), 4QXII^e (12:7-12) and 4QXII^a (14:18), and Greek fragments in 8HevXII gr (Zech. 9:1-5 only). Apart from plene variants in orthography, the only text-critical variation occurs in 4QXII^g Zech. 10:12 ("praise" *hll* in place of "walk" *hlk*), which is also reflected in the LXX. 8HevXII gr agrees with the MT against the LXX in Zech. 9:1—"to Yahweh are the eyes of mankind."

There are a number of divergences between the MT and the LXX, the more significant variations listed in Appendix 1. These variants can largely be explained as attempts by the LXX translator(s) to wrestle meaning from obscure vocabulary or imagery. For example, "Hadad-Rimmon in the plain of Megiddo" becomes "pomegranates (*rimmôn*) cut down (reading the verb *gd*' for the place name *mgdwn*) in the plain." The only variant that has found wide support among scholars is in Zech. 11:7, 11: reading "Canannite = merchant" (*kn*'*ny*) for "so the afflicted" (*kēn* '*ănîyēy*).

5.3 Genre, Composition, and Structure

Most scholars regard Zechariah 9–14 as a collection of somewhat disparate prophetic materials rather than a unified work, containing different streams of tradition reflecting competing perspectives—for example, with respect to human leadership in Israel and the fate of the nations.

Broadly speaking, there are two main theories about the compositional history of Zechariah 9–14—either that originally independent passages have been woven together by a redactor (or redactors) to form a literary mosaic or anthology, or that the text is the result of successive layers of redactional expansion.

On the first theory, the diversity is the result of the redactor adding "pessimistic" material (e.g., the various "shepherd" passages) to earlier "optimistic" blocks of material. For example, Redditt argues that the final redactor of Zechariah 9–14 wrote redactional "bridges" and "frames" to build "to his conclusion that the 'shepherds' had failed to rule well and that YHWH, not a Davidide, would rule in the future" (2012a:207). On the second theory, the diversity arises because each redactional stratum reflects the theological and temporal perspectives of a particular point in history. For example, Steck (1991:196–8) detects five redactional layers (9:1-10:2//10:3-11:3//11:4-13:9//Zechariah 14//addition of Zech. 12:1a) that span the period between 332 BCE and 190 BCE.

The superscription "Oracle" (*maśśā᾿*) occurs at the start of 9:1 and 12:1 and subdivides Zechariah 9–14 into two major units. There are notable differences between these two units. For example, "Israel" in Zechariah 9–11 encompasses the northern tribes (9:13, 10:6-12, 11:14), whereas Zech. 12:1 introduces an oracle "concerning Israel" in which Israel is limited in scope to Judah and Jerusalem (e.g., 12:2-7, 14:14, 14:21). Another difference is the phrase "on that day," which occurs sixteen times in Zechariah 12–14 with reference to an (eschatological?) day of distress and deliverance, compared to only two instances in Zechariah 9–11 (9:16, 11:11). On this basis, an earlier generation of scholars had partitioned the chapters into "Deutero-Zechariah" (9–11) and "Trito-Zechariah" (12–14) although this trend is less evident in more recent commentaries.

Not many scholars have been convinced by the argument of Floyd (2002) that the superscription *maśśā᾿* denotes a particular genre of prophecy involving the reinterpretation of past prophecies. (For a critique of Floyd, see

Boda 2006.) However, there is nonetheless a growing recognition that these chapters are some form of "scribal prophecy" (in German, *Schriftprophetie*) or "scribal interpretation" (*Schriftauslegung*)—that is, written compositions drawing on prophetic and other biblical traditions—whether or not this is signaled by maśśāʾ as a genre tag (cf. Weyde 2018).

The two oracles in Zechariah 9–14 can be further subdivided into a series of units. There is a degree of consensus as to the boundaries of the major units, as shown in the following table.

Zechariah 9–11			Zechariah 12–14		
9:1-17 10:1-12 11:1-3			11:4-17 12:1–13:6 13:7-9		14:1-21

Stade argued that Zech. 13:7-9 is out of place, having originally been located after Zech. 11:4-17. Stade's view quickly became the consensus. By 1912, Mitchell could write "the opinion that such a change has been made is widely held among biblical scholars" (1912:220). Reflecting the trend of biblical scholarship in the mid-twentieth century, the New English Bible relocated Zech. 13:7-9 to restore it to its presumed "original" location at the end of Zechariah 11. Since then, the pendulum of scholarly opinion has swung back in the opposite direction with the majority of scholars now interpreting Zech. 13:7-9 in the context of Zechariah 13.

Although there is general agreement about major units, there is little agreement about the subdivisions within these units, nor about how each unit relates to the other units in the oracle or whether there is an overarching structure.

Figure 5.1 The structure of Zechariah 9–14 (Lamarche)

A Judgment and salvation of neighbouring nations (9:1-8)

  B Arrival and description of the King (9:9-10)

    C Israel's war and victory (9:11–10:1)

      D Idolatry and judgment (10:2-3a)

    C' Israel's war and victory (10:3b–11:3)

  B' The shepherd rejected by the people (11:4-17)

    C" Israel's war and victory (12:1-9)

  B" Yahweh's representative pierced; mourning & purification (12:10–13:1)

      D' Idolatry and judgment (13:2-6)

  B'" Shepherd struck; judgment, purification, return to God (13:7-9)

    C" Israel's war and victory (14:1-15)

A' Judgment and salvation of all nations (14:16-21)

Figure 5.2 The structure of Zechariah 9–14 (Elliger)

9:1-8		9:11-17		10:3-12		11:4-16		12:1-13:6		14:1-21
	9:9-10		10:1-2		11:1-3		11:17		13:7-9	

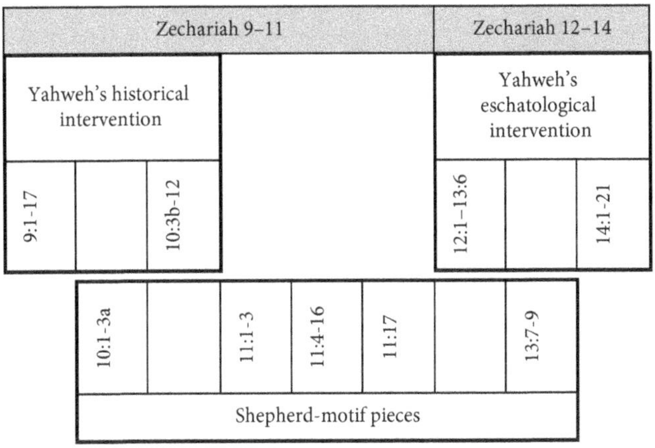

Zechariah 9–11		Zechariah 12–14
Yahweh's historical intervention		Yahweh's eschatological intervention

(9:1-17 · 10:3b-12 · 12:1–13:6 · 14:1-21)

(10:1-3a · 11:1-3 · 11:4-16 · 11:17 · 13:7-9)

Shepherd-motif pieces

Figure 5.3 The structure of Zechariah 9–14 (Boda)

Lamarche's (1961:112-13) elaborate chiastic structure for Zechariah 9–14 shown in Figure 5.1 has not found many supporters.

Elliger (1963:143-4) argued for an alternating pattern of larger units, which are linked by smaller subunits (9:9-10, 10:1-2, 11:1-3, 11:17, and 13:7-9) —see Figure 5.2.

Boda (2016:29) argues for a structure based on two pairs of originally disparate oracular units, which an editor has brought together by the addition of shepherd motif pieces at regular intervals (Figure 5.3).

Notwithstanding the lack of consensus on the overall structure, a growing number of scholars would broadly agree with Redditt that "Zech. 11:4-16 is the pivotal passage, standing between chapters of hope for a reunited Israel and Judah (and even a new king in 9:9-10) and depictions of future wars against Jerusalem and Judah (in 12:1-9 and 14:1-21), resulting ultimately in God's direct rulership not only over the city and Judah, but also the peoples of the rest of the world" (2012b:19).

"Intratextuality" and "Catchwords" (Stichwörter)

One of the features of Zechariah 9–14 that is relevant to our analysis of its structure is what Meyers and Meyers describe as "innertextuality" and what

I call "intratextuality"—the interwoven textual and thematic connections that link the various parts of Zechariah 9–14 together.

Butterworth (1992:278-290) catalogs the many verbal connections across Zechariah 9–14. To demonstrate this feature, Figure 5.4 lists the words or phrases, which are relatively unusual (less than fifty total instances in the Hebrew Bible) but which are in common between Zechariah 9 and 10.

While one or two of these phrases in common might not be significant, to have nine repeated in consecutive chapters cannot be accidental. There are similar patterns of linking words and phrases across all the chapters of the book. See further Meyers and Meyers (1993:33, 36–7).

These textual and thematic connections function as a series of hooks to link the different units together. However, there is an ongoing debate among scholars as to whether this points to an author who has artfully woven a broad range of material together (so Meyers and Meyers) or whether it is evidence of redaction, with "catchwords" (*Stichwörter* in German) introduced at the "seams" to join disparate material (see also §2.5). For example, Nogalski (1993a:228) argues that Zech. 9:16b-17 is an "addition which serves as a literary transition to the remaining chapters. This transition introduces the metaphor of the flock into the salvific motifs of 9:1-17, deliberately helping to prepare the dramatic reversal of the following chapters." A different example of the same approach is Redditt (2012a), who argues that 10:2-3a is a "redactional bridge" that was inserted into Zech. 10:1, 3b-12 to foreshadow the anti-shepherds in Zechariah 11.

My own view (similar to Meyers and Meyers) is that Zechariah 9–14 is an artfully constructed literary mosaic. Or, to reuse a metaphor that I have used elsewhere to describe Zechariah 1–8 (Stead 2009:127), Zechariah 9–14

Figure 5.4 Intratextual connections between Zechariah 9 and 10

Zechariah	Word or phrase	Instances
9:3/10:5	mud of the streets (*ṭîṭ ḥûṣôt*)	5×
9:5/10:5	confounded (*ybš hiphil*)	34×
9:6/10:11	pride (*gə'ôn*) of Philistia/Assyria	49×
9:8/10:4	oppressor/ruler (*ngś*)	23×
9:9/10:7	rejoice (*gyl*)	45×
9:10/10:4	battle bow (*qešet milḥāmā*)	2×
9:13/10:6-7	Judah/Ephraim (in contiguous verses)	43×
9:15/10:7	as with wine (*kəmô-yāyin*)	2×
9:16/10:2	like a flock (*kəṣō'n* or *kəmô-ṣō'n*)	8×

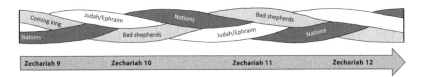

Figure 5.5 Interconnected thematic threads in Zechariah 9–11

is a tapestry, where thematic and textual threads have been carefully woven together into a single picture.

The Structure of Zechariah 9–11

This interthreaded structure is especially relevant for understanding the structure of Zechariah 9–11. The fact that there is no scholar consensus regarding the boundaries and transitions between the various subunits demonstrates that the subunits do not have sharp boundaries. In Zechariah 9–11, there are at least three threads that are woven together—a "nations" thread, a "salvation for Judah and Ephraim" thread (a sub-thread of which is their prosperity in the "land"), and a "leadership" thread (itself composed of two threads—"good shepherd" and "bad shepherds"). Figure 5.5 shows these threads as a three-stranded rope.

This diagram is not intended as an exact visualization of the structure of Zechariah 9–11, but as a representation of the way that thematic threads are interwoven in these chapters with overlapping themes at the transitions.

In light of this, the structure of Zechariah 9–11 can be represented as shown in Figure 5.6 (adapted from Butterworth 1992:290).

The Structure of Zechariah 12–14

As noted above, there is a shift in focus at Zechariah 12. There are no longer any explicit promises of salvation for Ephraim, the critique of bad shepherds does not continue (assuming that Zech. 13:7 describes a good shepherd), and the place of the nations in Yahweh's plan of salvation changes. There are also more structural markers.

Zechariah 12–14 can be subdivided into two units of similar length, Zech. 12:1a–13:9 and Zech. 14:1-21, with each subunit beginning with the Hebrew

Figure 5.6 The structure of Zechariah 9–11

		Nations	Leaders	People
9:1-8	Judgment for Judah's enemies (with a hint of salvation)	X		
9:9-10	Judah's righteous, saved, humble king comes		X	
9:11-17	Judgment for enemies and salvation for Judah/Ephraim	X		X
10:1-4	Judgment of corrupt leaders; provision of true leadership		X	
10:5-12	Strengthening for Judah/ Ephraim (+ judgment for enemies)	X		X
11:1-3	Judgment against bad leaders		X	
11:4-14	Judgment against bad leaders and stubborn people		X	X
11:15-17	Judgment on a worthless shepherd		X	

word *hinnēh* ("Behold!"). The structure outlined below takes the phrase "and it will be on that day" to be a key structural marker.

In Zechariah 12–13, this phrase occurs in Zech. 12:3, 12:9, 13:2, and 13:4, and a minor variation occurs in 13:1. A distinct oracle about the "sword" begins in 13:7. In Zechariah 14, this phrase occurs in 14:6, 14:8, and 14:13. Based on these observations, the following structure can be derived.

12:1a	Superscription
12:1-2	**Behold:** Jerusalem a cup that sends nations reeling
12:3-8	A day when the nations gather against Jerusalem
12:9-14	A day of repentance
13:1	A day of cleansing
13:2-3 (*)	A day when idolatry will be banished from the land
13:4-6 (*)	A day when false prophecy will cease
13:7-9	A day of the sword—refining judgment on the land
14:1-5	**Behold:** A day of Yahweh, of distress and battle
14:6-7	A day of new creation
14:8-12	A restored land
14:13-21	A day of transformation

* Zech. 13:2-6 will be treated as a single unit in the analysis below.

5.4 Inner-Biblical Allusions/ Intertextuality

One of the distinctive features of Zechariah 9–14 is that it draws heavily on earlier biblical texts and traditions. Scholars who have analyzed this aspect of Zechariah 9–14 include Stade (1881, 1882a, 1882b), Delcor (1952), Lutz (1968), Mason (1973), Ina Willi-Plein (1974), Person (1993), Larkin (1994), Schaefer (1995), Tai (1996), Nurmela (1996), and Lee (2015). Boda (2017:1-6) provides a helpful overview of the distinctive contributions of these scholars.

These scholars take different methodological approaches, which can be reflected in different terminology such as "inner-biblical exegesis" (e.g., Mason), "inner-biblical allusion" (e.g., Nurmela), "tradition history" (e.g., Lutz, Person, and Tai), and "intertextuality" (e.g., Lee). As Petersen notes (2003), these different methodological approaches reflect different interpretive claims and can lead to different conclusions.

The debate about whether Zechariah 9–14 depends on Isaiah 40–66 demonstrates this methodological divide. According to Nurmela (1996:163), whose method is based on rare lexical parallels, there are very few clear examples of textual connections between these two corpora. In contrast, Hanson (1979:390) argues that the "continuity [of Zech. 14] with earlier tradition is especially apparent in the repeated affinities with the prophecies of Second Isaiah and with the program of restoration in Isaiah 60–62."

In my view, a methodology that requires rare lexical parallels is too restrictive. For example, Zech. 9:10 repeats verbatim seven of the eight Hebrew words in Psalm 72:8 but replaces the verb *rdh* ("rule") with the noun *mōšel* ("dominion"). The seven shared words are all common words, and the only rare words are not in parallel between the two passages. A method based on rare lexical parallels (e.g., Nurmela) would not register a connection between Ps. 72:8 and Zech. 9:10.

The rich textual interplay in Zechariah 9–14 means that it is overly limiting to seek a connection with a single passage. For example, Zech. 13:3 is widely recognized to be some combination of Deut. 21:18-21 (a father and mother putting to death a rebellious son), Deut. 13:6-10 (the death penalty for leading others into apostasy), and/or Deut. 18:20-22 (the prophet who speaks presumptuously in Yahweh's name), even though the lexical parallels point to Jer. 14:14 as the best match.

Moreover, there are on occasions *no* significant lexical parallels, but there is still a clear thematic or tradition-historical parallel, such as the lying prophet's wounds in Zech. 13:6 and the self-inflicted wounds of the prophets of Baal in 1 Kgs 18:28, which is part of a Deuteronomic stream of tradition incorporating Deut. 14:1, Jer. 16:6, and Jer. 47:5.

I will use "intertextuality" as an umbrella term to cover the breadth of the textual and thematic connections found within Zechariah 9–14 (see further Stead 2009:16–39). Figure 5.7 lists the commonly recognized intertexts in Zechariah 9–14, based on the works of twelve scholars. To be included in the list, a connection had to be identified in at least two works. These works are identified using the following code in the final column.

Delcor 1952 = D; Jones 1962 = J; Mason 1973 = M [MP=possible]; Willi-Plein 1974 = W; Person 1991 = P; Meyers and Meyers 1993 = MM; Larkin 1994 = L; Schaefer 1995 = S, Nurmela 1996 = N [NL=likely, NP=possible]; Tai 1996= T, Lee 2015 = Lee

In Stead (2009), I identify three features of Zechariah 1–8 the intertextuality.

- *Textual mosaic*—it is highly allusive, made up of a mosaic of other texts.
- *Sustained allusion*—there are repeated references to "background" passages, which stretch across multiple passages.
- *Composite metaphors*—the simultaneous allusion to imagery from multiple source passages weaves hitherto distinct traditions together.

Figure 5.7 The intertexts of Zechariah 9–14

Zechariah 9–14 intertexts			
Zech. 9:2b-4	Tyre/wise/gold/ silver	Ezek. 28:4-8,18; Ezek. 27:27; 26:12	J,M,W,MM,NL,T,Lee
Zech. 9:5	see/fear/tremble	Jer. 5:20-25	T,Lee
Zech. 9:5-7	Ashkelon, Gaza, Ekron, Ashdod	Amos 1:6-8 / Jer. 25:20 / Zeph. 2:4-7	J,M,W,MM,L
Zech. 9:8	Yahweh encamped	Isa. 29:3 ; Zech. 2:8-9; Zech. 7:14	M,W,NL,L
Zech. 9:9	rejoice daughter Jerusalem	Zech. 2:10, Zeph. 3:14	M,W,MM,T,L,Lee

Zechariah 9–14 intertexts			
Zech. 9:9	donkey	Gen. 49:10-11	D, MM, L, Lee
Zech. 9:10	rule/sea/river/earth	Ps. 72:8	J, M, MM, T, L, Lee
Zech. 9:11	blood of the covenant	Exod. 24:8	J, W, MM, T, LP, Lee
Zech. 9:11	waterless pit	Gen. 37:24; Jer. 38:6	MP, W, P, MM, L, Lee
Zech. 9:12	restoring double	Jer. 16:18 / Isa. 40:2 / Isa. 61:1, 7	D, J, M, W, MM, L
Zech. 9:15	Yahweh as fence	Isa. 31:5	N, Lee
Zech. 9:16-17	jewels of a crown; beauty	Isa. 62:3	D, MP, MM, NP
Zech. 10:1-2	Ask for rain, lying diviners	Jer. 14:1–15:4 esp. 14:14 and 14:22	M, W, P, MM, N, T, L, Lee
Zech. 10:3-10	against the shepherd, attend to, gather, be many, Judah and Ephraim saved	Jer. 23:1-8	M, W, P, MM, N, T, LP, Lee
Zech. 10:3-10	bad shepherds	Ezek. 34:1-5	D, M, W, MM, L, Lee
Zech. 10:4	leaders going out from him	Jer. 30:21	J, MP, W, P, N, Lee
Zech. 10:6, 9	answer/mercy/be their God	Hos. 2:21-23 [MT 23-25]	W, T, Lee
Zech. 10:8-10	whistle/Egypt/Assyria	Isa. 5:25-26; 7:18; Isa. 11:11-16	D, J, N, T, LP, Lee
Zech. 10:8	sowing of Israel and multiplication of race	Jer. 31:27 + Jer. 30:19-20	D, P, T, LP
Zech. 10:8	for I have loved them; I have redeemed them	Jer. 31:3b, 10-11	D, Lee
Zech. 10:9	remember from afar	Jer. 51:50	T, Lee
Zech. 10:10	there is no room for	Josh. 17:16	T, Lee
Zech. 10:11	strike the waters	Isa. 11:11-12, 15-16	J, N, Lee
Zech. 11:1-2	cedars/Lebanon/oaks/Bashan	Isa. 2:12-13	J, W, NL, L

Zechariah 9–14 intertexts			
Zech. 11:3	roaring lions	Jer. 25:34-38 + Jer. 2:15; 4:7	D,J,M,W,P,MM,N,T,L
Zech. 11:3	thicket of the Jordan	Jer. 12:5; Jer. 49:19 = 50:44	J,W,P
Zech. 11:4	sheep for the slaughter	Jer. 12:3; cf. Jer. 7:32 & 19:6	D,J,M,W,P
Zech. 11:5	bad shepherds	Ezek. 34 esp. vv.2-3	M,W,MM,N,L
11:7/10/14	two staffs	Ezek. 37:15-17	D,M,W,MM,N,T,L
Zech. 11:8-9	whoever/die/ destroyed	Jer. 15:2, 6; Jer. 11:9	D,P,MM
Zech. 11:16	bad shepherds	Ezek. 34:4; 34:14; 34:3; 34:10; 37:16	MM,N,T,L
Zech. 12:1-2	Creation + cup of judgment	Isa. 51:13-15, 17, 22-23	M,W,MM,NL,T
Zech. 12:4	smite/panic/ madness/ blindness	Deut. 28:28	D,J,M,W,P,MM,N,T,L
Zech. 12:10	pour out (my) spirit	Ezek. 39:29	W,N,T
Zech. 12:10	mourn an only child	Jer. 6:26 (cf. Amos 8:10)	MM,L
Zech. 12:10	lament over pierced one	Isa. 53:5	J,LP
Zech. 12:11	plain of Megiddo/ Josiah	2 Chron. 35:20-24 (cf. 2 Kgs 23:29-30)	J,P,MM,L
Zech. 13:1-2	impurity/sin/ cleanse/ pour out	Ezek. 36:17,22-32 [+ Num. 19:9]	D,J,M,W,MM,N,T,L
Zech. 13:2	in that day … idols … not remembered	Hos. 2:16-17 [MT 18-19]	W,N,T
Zech. 13:3	prophet lying in Yahweh's name	Jer. 14:14, Deut 13:2-6, Jer. 29:23	J,P,NL
Zech. 13:4	hairy mantle	Gen. 25:25, 2 Kgs 1:8 + 2:8	P,MM,T,L
Zech. 13:5	I am not a prophet	Amos 7:14	D,J,M,P,W,MM,T,LP

Zechariah 9–14 intertexts			
Zech. 13:6	prophet's wounds	1 Kgs 18:28	J,P,T
Zech. 13:7	Yahweh's sword/ people/testing	Ezek. 21:9-13, Ezek. 21:30 [MT 35]	D,MP
Zech. 13:8	Two thirds/ one third	Ezek. 5:11-12	D,J,M,MM,N,T,L
Zech. 13:8-9	turn hand against, refine your dross	Isa. 1:25	M,N
Zech. 14:2	Gather nations against Jerusalem	Ezek. 38:1-6, 16; Joel 3:2 [4:2], cf. Zech. 12:1	J,MP,(W),MM,S,T
Zech. 14:1, 2	plunder/spoil	Ezek. 38:12-13	MM,S
Zech. 14:2	houses plundered/ women ravished	Isa. 13:16	W,MM,S,T
Zech. 14:4	Mt of Olives	Ezek. 11:23; 43:2	J,M,W,MM,S,NP,T,L
Zech. 14:4-5	mountains moved	Ezek. 38:19-22	D,J,MM,S
Zech. 14:6	no light	Isa. 13:9-10 / Amos 5:18 / Zeph. 1:15	S,T
Zech. 14:7	evening time there shall be light	Isa. 60:19-20	D,J,W,S
Zech. 14:8	River from Jerusalem	Ezek. 47:1-12; Joel 3:18 [MT 4:18]	J,M,W,MM,S,N,T
Zech. 14:9	Yahweh is one	Deut. 4:6	J,M,W,P,MM,S,L
Zech. 14:10	Corner Gate, Tower of Hananel, etc.	Jer. 31:38-40	D,M,W,P,S,T,L
Zech. 14:13	enemies kill each other	Ezek. 38:21	MM,S,L
Zech. 14:16	pilgrimage of the nations	Isa. 60:5-21	D,J,T
Zech. 14:16	pilgrimage of the nations	Isa. 2:1-4‖Mic. 4:1-4; Zech. 8:20-23	J,M,W,S,NL,T
Zech. 14:16	Nations go up to worship Yahweh	Isa. 66:18-24	D,J,(W),S,N(↔),L
Zech. 14:20	"Holy to Yahweh"	Exod. 28:36	M,MM,S,L

These three features are also present in Zechariah 9–14.

Firstly, the breadth of textual connections identified in the table above demonstrates Zechariah 9–14's **textual mosaic**. Mason (1973:303) identifies "allusive word-play" as a key feature of Zechariah 9–14.

Secondly, the combined analysis of Person (1991:105–16), Schaefer (1995:72–6), and Lee (2015:241) demonstrates that Zechariah 9–14 contains **sustained allusions** to the following "background" passages: Psalm 72, Exod. 24:3-11, Deuteronomy 28, Isaiah 2–4, Isaiah 13, Isa. 30:18-33, Jer. 14:1–15:4, Jer. 23:1-8, Jeremiah 25, Jeremiah 30–31, Ezekiel 34, Ezekiel 36–37, Ezekiel 38–39, Ezek. 47:1-12, Zephaniah 1, and (perhaps) Joel 4.

Zechariah 9–14 often weaves together multiple traditions to create new **composite metaphors**. For example, in Zech. 10:3-11, the sustained allusion to Jer. 23:1-8 is interwoven with allusions to Ezekiel, Isaiah, Hosea, and other parts of Jeremiah, as shown in Figure 5.8.

The recognition that composite metaphors are a feature of Zechariah 9–14 makes it reasonable to posit (for example) that Zech. 13:3 is some combination of Deut. 21:18-21 (a father and mother putting to death a rebellious son), Deut. 13:6-10 (the death penalty for leading others into apostasy), Deut. 18:20-22 (the prophet who speaks presumptuously in Yahweh's name), and/or Jer. 14:14 (lying in Yahweh's name), without having to choose one expression of this tradition over the other. Similarly, we can connect the lying prophet's wounds in Zech. 13:6 with the self-inflicted wounds of the prophets of Baal in 1 Kgs 18:28, recognizing this to be part of a Deuteronomic stream of tradition incorporating Deut. 14:1, Jer. 16:6, and Jer. 47:5.

Figure 5.8 Interwoven intertexts in Zechariah 10

Zechariah 10	Jeremiah 23	Other
[3] My anger is hot **against the shepherds**, and I will **attend to** the *he-goats*; for the Lord of hosts **attends to** his *flock*,	[23:1 "Woe"] [2] **against the shepherds** "… You have not **attended to** my flock. Behold, I will **attend to** you".	Ezek. 34:17: he goats Ezek. 34:12: flock
[4] **From him shall come** the **cornerstone**, from him the **tent peg**, from him the **battle bow**, from him every ruler-all of them together		Jer. 30:21: leaders "from him" Isa. 28:16: cornerstone Isa. 22:23: tent-peg Zech. 9:10: battle bow

6a I will strengthen the house of **Judah**, and I will **save** the house of **Joseph** because	6 In his day, **Judah** will be **saved**, and **Israel** will dwell securely.	
6b I have **compassion** on them, and they shall be as though I had not rejected them, for I am **Yahweh their God** and I will **answer** them.		Hos. 2:23-25— compassion, answer, "You are my God"
8 I will **whistle** for them and		Isa. 5:26; 7:18— whistle
8 **gather** them in, for I have redeemed them, and they shall be as **many** as they were before.	3 Then **I will gather** the remnant of my flock out of all the countries where I have driven them… and they shall be fruitful and **be many**.	
9 Though I **sowed them** among the nations, yet **in far countries they shall remember me**, and with their children they shall live and return		Hos. 2:23—Yahweh sowing people Jer. 51:50— remember the Lord from afar
10 I will bring them home from the **land of Egypt**, and gather them from **Assyria**	7 brought up the people of Israel out of the **land of Egypt** … 8 brought the descendants of Israel out of the **north country** …	Isa. 11:11-16—*gathered from Egypt and Assyria*
11 He shall pass through the sea of troubles and strike down the waves of the sea, and all the depths of the Nile shall be dried up.		Isa. 11:15—*strike the river and cause it to dry up.*

There does not appear to be a significant difference in intertextual technique between Zechariah 9–11 and Zechariah 12–14—both are *textual mosaics* involving *sustained allusions* and *composite metaphors* with a similar number of allusions in each section. We shall return to this point when we come to the question of authorship (see §5.6).

In addition to the connections with other biblical books, there are also striking connections between Zechariah 1–8 and 9–14. Nurmela (1996:213–30) registers seven lexical connections. Furthermore, as will be discussed in the next section, there is "significant thematic continuity" (Mason) and notable "elements of congruity" (Childs) between the two corpora.

5.5 Relationship with Zechariah 1–8

The relationship between Zechariah 1–8 and Zechariah 9–14 is connected with the question of authorship (see §5.6).

It is common ground that there are notable differences in form, structure, focus, tone, and rhetorical devices between Zechariah 1–8 and Zechariah 9–14, some of which are summarized in Figure 5.9.

It is because of these elements of discontinuity that most scholars see Zechariah 1–8 and 9–14 as discrete units. An alternative, minority view

Figure 5.9 Differences between Zechariah 1–8 and 9–14

	Zechariah 1–8	Zechariah 9–14
Structural devices	Dating formulas, vision framework	"Oracle" (maśśāʾ) 9:1 and 12:1
Form	A "sermonic" framework (1:1-6 + 7:1–8:23) around 8 vision reports with oracles and two sign-acts	Oracular prose and oracular poetry + a twofold sign-act
Role of the prophet	The prophet Zechariah is central to sermons, vision reports, and oracles	The prophet disappears from view (except 11:4-17)
Focus	Temple, priesthood, cultic worship	9–11—Israel 12–14—Jerusalem
Tone	Optimistic	Mixed-pessimism and hope
Rhetorical devices		
Interrogatives	26 times	1 (Zech. 13:6)
Thus says Yahweh of hosts	17 times	0
Thus says Yahweh	2 times	1 (Zech. 11:4)
The word of Yahweh (of hosts) to …	9 times	0

argues for a structural connection between the units, taking Zech. 7:1–8:23 to be an introduction for the two oracles in 9–14. For example, Sweeney argues that Zechariah 7–8 declares that "the times for mourning are to be considered as a time for rejoicing as the nations will now recognize YHWH in Jerusalem as the Temple is rebuilt" and that Zechariah 9–14 "spell[s] out the process by which this scenario is to take place" (2000:566–7; see similarly Conrad 1999). This approach has not persuaded many, because the dating in 7:1 (the fourth year of Darius) is an unlikely context for the oracles in Zechariah 9–14.

A different context would appear to be the best explanation for differences in content. Zechariah 1–8 is written to the first generation of returnees to assure them of the imminent—but partial—fulfillment of the promises that Yahweh made through the earlier prophets. Zechariah 9–14 is written to a subsequent generation, to explain that the ultimate fulfillment of these promises was still some way off in the future, and to explain that the deferral of their hopes is because of the failed leadership (bad shepherds).

Notwithstanding the formal and stylistic differences between Zechariah 1–8 and 9–14, scholars note significant thematic continuity between them. For example, Mason identifies five lines of tradition from Zechariah 1–8 that continue in Zechariah 9–14—"the prominence of the Zion tradition; the divine cleansing of the community; universalism; the appeal to the earlier prophets; and the provision of leadership as a sign of the new age" (1976:227; similarly Childs 1979:482–3, Butterworth 1992:291–6).

Another aspect to the continuity between Zechariah 1–8 and 9–14 is that both corpora exhibit a very similar intertextual technique (as discussed above). One example of this is that there are sustained allusions to a similar set of passages. The highlighted references in the table below indicate the commonalities.

5.6 Authorship

The majority view of current scholarship is that Zechariah the prophet could not have been the author of Zechariah 9–14. Nogalski summarizes the argument against Zecharian authorship as follows.

> Since the end of the nineteenth century, chapters 9–14 have been treated as having a different author and date than chapters 1–8. The differences in

Sustained allusions in Zechariah 1–8 (Stead 2009)	Sustained allusions in Zechariah 9–14 (see above)
Deuteronomy 28–30	Deuteronomy 28
Exodus 25–27	Exod. 24:3-11
2 Samuel 7	
Isaiah 2, Isaiah 12–14, Isaiah 40–55	Isaiah 2–4, Isaiah 13, Isa. 30:18-33
Jeremiah 7, Jeremiah 12–14, Jeremiah 30–33, Jeremiah 48–51	Jer. 14:1–15:4, Jer. 23:1-8, Jeremiah 25, Jeremiah 30–31
Ezekiel 38–39, Ezekiel 40–48	Ezekiel 34, Ezekiel 36–37, Ezekiel 38–39, Ezek. 47:1-12
Lamentations 2	
Joel 1–2	Joel 3 [MT 4]
	Zephaniah 1
	Psalm 72

outlook are too stark in terms of the general message, the forms, the style, and the intellectual presumptions to be the work of one person.

(2011:807)

A typical example of this view is Mitchell (1912:234)—"It is clear that, if Zechariah wrote the first eight chapters of the book called by his name, he cannot have written [Zechariah 9–11]. They constituted an elaborate poem; he in his undoubted writings never attempted to put together a dozen lines."

In my view, the evidence about writing style is more ambiguous than Mitchell allows. If we allow that Zechariah 1–8 could have been written by Zechariah, then this demonstrates his stylistic versatility, in that he is able to alternate between sermonic prose, vision reports, oracles, and sign-act accounts. Notably, the poetic oracles such as Zech. 2:6-13 [MT 2:10-17] are highly allusive (see, e.g., Boda 2008) and are arguably emerging examples of "scribal prophecy," which we see more fully developed in Zechariah 9–14. It would seem to be an open question as to whether Zechariah himself could have written Zechariah 9–14 in later life. As we have seen, Zechariah 9–14 is connected to (or perhaps responding to) Zechariah 1–8 in a way that (say) Malachi is not. How best to account for this connection?

As to the question of authorship, there are two main alternatives. The first is that Zechariah 9–14 was written by "disciples" of Zechariah, who were thoroughly immersed in Zechariah's intertextual techniques (and apparently had the same set of favorite intertexts), who were shaped by many of the same theological concerns and who further developed Zechariah's nascent "scribal prophecy" approach, but who were also shaped by a different social (and theological?) context that is reflected in the emerging apocalyptic eschatology (see below) in these chapters. The second alternative is that Zechariah 9–14 was composed by Zechariah himself in the first half of the fifth century BCE, perhaps three or more decades after completing Zechariah 1–8, and that the differences in theological perspective reflect Zechariah's own development over time.

The debate about authorship is not resolvable on the evidence available to us. It is not unlike the debate in New Testament scholarship as to whether the author of the fourth gospel could have been the author of the book of Revelation, given the marked differences in style and theological outlook.

5.7 Zechariah 9–14 and the Emergence of Apocalyptic

The year 1979 saw the publication of two seminal works focused on "apocalyptic."

The first was as special edition of *Semeia*, edited by J. J. Collins, entitled "Apocalypse: The Morphology of a Genre," which grew out of the work of the "Apocalypse Group" of the Society of Biblical Literature to define the genre of apocalypse. The group's definition, which has been widely accepted, is as follows:

> An apocalypse is a genre of revelatory literature with a narrative framework in which a revelation is mediated by an otherworldly being to a human recipient, disclosing a transcendent reality which is both temporal, insofar as it envisages eschatological salvation, and spatial, insofar as it involves another, supernatural world.
>
> (1979:9)

In the introduction, Collins argues that

> the label "apocalyptic eschatology" should be reserved for the eschatology found in apocalypses or recognized by analogy with them … The transcendent nature of apocalyptic eschatology looks beyond this world to another. The forms of salvation are diverse, exaltation to the heavens or renewal of the earth, but in all cases they involve a radically different type

of human existence, in which all the constraints of the human condition, including death, are transcended.

(1979:4, 10)

The second seminal work was Paul Hanson's *Dawn of Apocalyptic*. Hanson, building on Plöger (1968), argues for a sociopolitical explanation for the emergence of apocalyptic, arising from the "bitter struggle between two groups for control of the restoration cult" (1979:290). The "visionaries" represented the continuation of the prophetic tradition, whereas the "hierocrats" represented the priestly tradition: the religious establishment. Hanson argues "that apocalyptic eschatology is the mode assumed by the prophetic tradition once it had been transferred to a new and radically altered setting in the post-exilic community" (1979:10). The visionaries had become disillusioned with the historical realm and looked instead to the cosmic realm of the Yahweh, the divine warrior (1979:12).

Hanson argues that Zechariah 9–14 in particular represents a progressive development of apocalyptic eschatology and that "the essentials of apocalyptic eschatology are all present [in Zechariah 14]" (1979:396).

We noted in the previous chapter that, although the visions in Zechariah 1–6 exhibit many of the formal features of a type of literature called "apocalyptic" (visions of the heavenly realm, heavenly beings, animals, and number symbolism, etc.), there is no evidence of an apocalyptic eschatology.

Zechariah 9–14 is the reverse—it lacks the formal features of apocalyptic, but there is a *developing* apocalyptic eschatology, especially in Zechariah 14 (Collins 1979:29). However, Zechariah 9–14 is best described not as "apocalyptic," but as prophetic oracles with traces of an apocalyptic eschatology.

5.8 Overview of Zechariah 9–14— Key Issues

Key intertexts are marked with []—see §2.5 and §5.4.

The three units in **Zechariah 9** are linked by a paradox of peace through warfare and victory through near defeat. The chapter begins with Yahweh fighting for his people, bringing their enemies into subjugation. In Zech.

9:10, Yahweh promises, "I will take away the chariots from Ephraim and the war-horses from Jerusalem, and the battle bow will be broken." Yet the chapter ends with the people in battle against their enemies, until finally delivered by Yahweh (see vv. 14-16). At the heart of the chapter is the king who comes to Jerusalem, riding on a donkey (9:9), who is the personification of "victory through apparent defeat." The paradox of the suffering king of Zech. 9:9 establishes the paradigm for Yahweh's people as a whole—Yahweh will give them the ultimate victory but via the way of suffering and near defeat. Zechariah 12–14 in particular will return to this theme.

9:1-8 Judgment for Judah's Enemies (with a Hint of Salvation)

The cities named in 9:1-7 are located in three regions—Aram (Hadrach, Damascus, and Hamath), Phoenicia (Tyre and Sidon), and Philistia (Ekron, Ashdod, Ashkelon, and Gaza)—see Figure 5.10.

As noted in §5.1, many scholars have sought to interpret this unit against the historical background of various military campaigns—whether Assyrian, Babylonian, Persian, or Greek (see Boda 2016:531 for details)—with Alexander's campaign in 332 BCE being the preferred option. However, no military campaign is an exact fit, and these approaches (which focus on human military endeavor) tend to miss the point of this unit, which is about Yahweh's deliverance of his people.

The first subunit (9:1-2a) is about Aram, of which Damascus was the chief city. The location of the region of Hadrach is unknown, but the reference to Hamath in v. 2 helps to localize it. Hamath was the idealized northern-most boundary of the Promised Land (cf. Josh. 13:5; 2 Chron. 8:3; 2 Kgs 14:28). These three place names collectively represent a substantial region in Aram (=Syria).

Scholars are divided as to whether an amendment to the MT is necessary in v. 1. The MT reads *la*YHWH *ʿēyn* *ʾādām* (lit. "to Yahweh [is] the eye of Adam/man"). The LXX inverts the word order ("The Lord looks upon men"). The RSV translation reflects various proposals (see, e.g., Mitchell 1912:263; Rudolph 1976:167–8) to amend *ʿēyn* "eye" to *ʿārēy* "cities" and *ʾādām* "Adam/man" to *ʾărām* "Aram", resulting in the translation "to Yahweh are the cities of Aram." However, the MT makes sense as is, especially if Larkin (1994:58–9) is correct that Zech. 9:1 alludes to the oracle against Damascus in *[Isaiah 17:7]*, which describes a day on which "man (*ʾādām*)

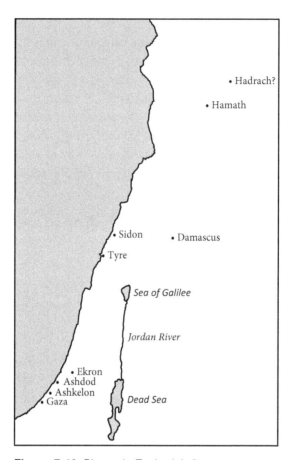

Figure 5.10 Places in Zechariah 9

will look to his maker, and his eyes (ʿēyn) will look to the Holy One of Israel." Nonetheless, whether this verse says "the eyes of mankind and the all the tribes of Israel to Yahweh" (as per the MT) or "the cities of Aram and all the tribes of Israel are to Yahweh" (amended), the net result is similar, in that either way it declares Yahweh's sovereignty beyond the borders of Israel.

The fate of Aram in this oracle is a matter of debate. Most take 9:1-2a as the word of Yahweh *against* these three places and that reference to its "resting place" in Damascus (9:1) is taken negatively (cf. Zech. 6:8). However, Zech. 9:1 is more naturally translated, "The word of Yahweh is *in* the land of Hadrach and Damascus is its resting place." On this reading, 9:1-2a anticipates the restoration of the dimensions of the Promised Land to its maximal dimensions with Yahweh's word present even in the northern-most parts of the land (cf. Ezek. 47:16-17).

The next subunit, Zech. 9:2b-4, describes the fate of Tyre (and Sidon, by implication). This section echoes Ezekiel's prophecy against Tyre in Ezekiel 26–28 (see esp. *[Ezek. 28:4-8, 18; Ezek. 26:12; 27:27]*). The Lord (*'ădōnāy*) will dispossess Tyre of her amassed wealth and strike down her famed power on the sea, and the city will be consumed by fire, thereby subduing Israel's historic enemies.

The third subunit, Zech. 9:5-7, is focused on four Philistine cities. The first two verses echo typical prophecies against the Philistines, especially *[Amos 1:6-8, Jer. 25:20, and Zeph. 2:4-7]*, but the final verse takes a surprising turn. Whereas the previous prophecies promised no inhabitants would remain (e.g., Amos 1:8, Zeph. 2:5, Jer. 25:27), Yahweh promises in Zech. 9:7 to purify a remnant of the Philistines, who will become incorporated into the nation of Israel.

Yahweh's promise to subdue/remove/convert external threats in 9:1-7 is expressed positively in v. 8—Yahweh will "encamp" at Jerusalem to protect it against invasion. This inverts the imagery of *[Isa. 29:3]*, the only other instance of Yahweh "encamping" at Jerusalem. Zech. 9:8 repeats in different words the promise of *[Zech. 2:8-9]* that Jerusalem will be protected because of Yahweh's presence.

9:9-10 Judah's Righteous, Saved, Humble King Comes

This unit uses a series of intertexts to describe a coming king. Zech. 9:9a is strongly reminiscent of *[Zech. 2:10]*, but with a twist. In Zech. 2:10 (and cf. Isa. 12:6 and Zeph. 3:14), Jerusalem is to rejoice because of the coming of Yahweh to dwell in her midst, whereas in Zech. 9:9, the call to rejoice is because a human king is coming to Jerusalem. It is unexpected that this human king is accorded the same praise as if it were Yahweh himself arriving.

The credentials of this king are informed by another intertext in Zech. 9:10b, which is a near-quotation from *[Ps. 72:8]*. This coming king will rule over an idealized Davidic kingdom, for which David prayed in Psalm 72.

Between these two intertexts, which have strong messianic connotations, sits another very different description of this king—a king who is "righteous," "having been saved," and "humbled" (=afflicted). These words are not an allusion to one specific text but rather a fusion of the tradition of the suffering

David in the Psalms with Isaiah's suffering servant (see Stead 2013, cf. Mason 1973:46–52). The reference to the donkey in 9:9 is better understood not as an allusion Gen. 49:10-11 but to the humiliation of David in *[2 Samuel 15–16]*. As such, Zechariah 9 depicts a David-like figure, who having been afflicted has been saved by Yahweh and brought back to Jerusalem on the same humble donkey. Yahweh will take away the weapons of war, and the coming king will proclaim peace to the nations (9:10).

9:11-17 Judgment for Enemies and Salvation for Judah/Ephraim

In the third unit, the focus shifts from the coming king to his people, who are promised release and restoration (vv. 11-12) and victory over enemies (vv. 13-15) that ushers in a day of salvation (vv. 16-17).

The people will be released from a waterless pit—not a literal dry well (Gen. 37:24; Jer. 38:6) but that which is described in *[Jer. 2:13]*. According to Jer. 2:13, the people have committed two evils—they have forsaken Yahweh, the spring of living water, and have dug their own waterless cisterns. For these two evils, Yahweh will doubly repay their iniquity (Jer. 16:18, cf. 16:11). Zech. 9:12 completes a fourfold chain of *["double" promises]*. Double judgment declared (Jer. 16:18), led to Jerusalem receiving the double (Isa. 40:2), which is reversed by a promise of double blessing (Isa. 61:7). Zech. 9:12 announces the imminent fulfillment of Isaiah 61—"today, Yahweh restores the double" (Zech. 9:12).

Zech. 9:13-15 describes both Yahweh fighting *through* his people (using Judah and Ephraim as his bow and arrow) (v. 13) and Yahweh fighting *for* his people (v. 14) and protecting them (v. 15) *[Isa. 31:5; see also Zech. 12:8]*. The people's experience is like King David's experience in *[Psalm 18]*, where Yahweh fights both *through* David (18:34-35) and *for* David; Yahweh is David's fortress (18:2, cf. Zech. 9:12). Yahweh "soared on the wings of the wind" (18:11), "shot his arrows and scattered [the enemies], great bolts of lightning and routed them" (18:14), etc. Yahweh will appear and march in the storms of the south against his enemies (cf. Jer. 30:23) while shielding his people. "Overcoming with sling stones" alludes to David's unlikely victory over Goliath *[1 Sam. 17:50]*. David's experience of salvation has become the paradigm for the nation as a whole.

Zech. 9:16-17 describes the day of salvation following victory in battle. Zech. 9:16 repeats the word for "save" used in Zech. 9:9—the king who "has been saved" establishes the pattern for the people—Yahweh will "save" his flock. The people will then shine like the jewels in a crown *[cf. Isa. 62:3]* and thrive on grain and new wine.

10:1-4 Judgment of Corrupt Leaders; Provision of True Leadership

This unit begins with an exhortation to ask Yahweh for rain (10:1), instead of turning to idols and divination for rain (10:2) *[Jer. 14:22]*. Because the people have been led astray by falsehood and empty dreams, they are like sheep without a shepherd (10:2) *[Num. 27:16-17, 1 Kgs 22:17]*. Yahweh is angry at the "shepherds" of Israel because of this *[Ezek. 34:1-10]*. Repeating a word play from Jeremiah *[Jer. 23:2]*, Yahweh announces that he will "take care of" the shepherds (leaders) in order to "take care of" his flock (10:3).

This will involve replacing the bad shepherds of the house of Judah with a new kind of leadership—"From him" (i.e., from Judah, not from Yahweh) will come a corner, from him a tent peg, from him a bow of war, from him every taskmaster, together (10:4). The fourfold repetition of "from him" alludes to *[Jer. 30:21]*, which promises that prince and ruler would come "from him" (= emerge from "Jacob").

There are no particular messianic overtones to the four types of leader listed in v. 14. The word translated "corner" refers to various types of leaders (e.g., Judg. 20:2, 1 Sam. 14:28, and Isa. 19:13). A "tent-peg" is used metaphorically in Isa. 22:22-23 of Eliakim son of Hilkiah as palace steward. The "battle bow" is not used elsewhere as a metaphor for a leader, but it is an obvious image of military strength (cf. Zech. 9:10). "Taskmaster" is usually translated in the negative sense of oppressor. These metaphors describe a variety of "ordinary" leaders (as distinct from the king promised in 9:9) whom Yahweh will provide for his people to replace the bad shepherds.

10:5-12 Strengthening for Judah/Ephraim (± Judgment for Enemies)

The theme of "strengthening" links this unit together, with the verb or its cognate noun occurring in 10:5, 10:6, 10:7, and 10:12. The leaders raised up from within Judah (identified in 10:4) will become "like strong men" (10:5), whom Yahweh will make victorious in battle. Yahweh will "strengthen the house of Judah" (10:6) and save the house of Joseph, who will also "become like strong men" (10:7). All those who return from the nations in which they have been scattered will be "strengthened in Yahweh" (10:12).

This unit repeats a number of the themes of 9:11-17—salvation for both Judah and Ephraim, Yahweh giving his people victory in battle, and release and return from exile. It also repeats a theme of 9:1-8, of a nation so populous that it overflows its traditional borders, in this case spilling into Gilead (located to the East of the Jordan River) and Lebanon (to the North of Israel). In contrast to 9:1-8 and 9:11-17, the theme of judgment of enemies is only present in an incidental way—the vanquished foes in 10:5 are unnamed and merely demonstrate the strength of Judah.

In 10:5-12, the dominant imagery is drawn from Hosea 2 and Isaiah 7–11. Zech. 10:6 echoes the key words from *[Hos. 2:21-23]* that promise Yahweh's "compassion," Yahweh "answering," and the restoration of the covenant relationship between Yahweh and this house of Israel. Zech. 10:8 uses the imagery of "whistling" for Egypt and Assyria from *[Isa. 7:18]* but with the opposite effect—it is God's people (rather than the nations) who are being signaled in order to gather them in from Egypt and Assyria. Zech. 10:10-11 pictures Israel's redemption as a second Exodus, echoing many of the themes of *[Isa. 11:12-16]*.

11:1-3 Judgment against Bad Leaders

Zech. 11:1-3 returns to the theme of "bad shepherds" introduced in 10:1-3. In 10:3, Yahweh announces that he will punish the shepherds. Zech. 11:1-3 depicts this.

Scholars are divided as to whether the cedars of Lebanon and the oaks of Bashan in Zech. 11:1-2 refer to literal trees, metaphorically weeping because of agricultural destruction, or whether they are metaphoric for proud leaders. In my view, *[Isa. 2:12-18]* and *[Jer. 25:36-38]* help to resolve this question. As in Isaiah 2, so also in Zechariah 11, the "cedars of Lebanon" and the "oaks of Bashan" are metaphors referring to arrogant human leaders (Isa. 2:17). The wailing cedars and oaks in Zech. 11:2 represent leaders who wail because of the destruction of the land. They are the same group as the wailing shepherds in 11:3, who (as in Jer. 25:26-38) are the leaders of the flock who cry out because Yahweh is destroying their pasture (="the land has become a waste," Jer. 25:38). Zech. 11:1-3 depict how Yahweh's judgment on the shepherds of Israel led to the desolation of the whole land.

11:4-14 Judgment against Bad Leaders and Stubborn People

A key issue in this unit is the relationship to the Ezekiel's sign-act in *[37:15-28]*. The majority of current scholarship takes Zech. 11:4-17 to be the sequel to Ezekiel's act, and therefore a modification—or indeed, a repudiation—of the promise in Ezekiel 37 of the reunification of Judah and Ephraim under a Davidic King. Some take it be a critique of contemporary leadership in the Persian Era (e.g., Hanson 1979:241–2; Redditt 1993:676–86). Others interpret this passage against the context of the third century BCE (e.g., Mitchell 1912:307) or second century BCE (e.g., Oesterley 1932:258). Some Christian commentators, noting the allusion to Zechariah 11 in Matt. 27:9, interpret this to be a prophecy about Christ and the destruction of Jerusalem in 70 CE (e.g., Keil 1961:371).

The other approach, which although a minority position, has much to commend it, understands this sign act to be portraying the past, and as such is a "prequel" (rather than a sequel) to Ezekiel 37 (see Meyer 1977:225–40; Meyers and Meyers 1993:248–304; Merrill 1994:287–301; Webb 2003:147–52; Petterson 2009:181–93; Stead 2011). On this view, the sign-act depicts how Yahweh shepherded his people circa 586 BCE, in light of the sins of his under-shepherds and his flock. Because the leaders had led the people astray and the flock had rejected Yahweh as their shepherd, he removed the leaders and allowed his people to be exiled or killed. As to the identity of "the three shepherds" who were removed in "one month," most taking this approach suggest that this may refer to the last three kings of Judah (Jehoiakim, Jehoiachin, and Zedekiah), taking "one month" to be figurative for a relatively short period. Alternatively, see Stead (2011) for the argument that the "three shepherds" refer to the offices of king, priest, and prophet, which were cut off in the space of exactly one month in 586 BCE (see Jer. 52:6-27).

[Ezekiel 34] is essential to understanding Zech. 11:4-17 (i.e., this unit and the next). In Ezekiel 34, the shepherd metaphor describes both divine and human leadership. Yahweh is the true shepherd of Israel (Ezek. 34:11-23), and he appoints under-shepherds to care for his flock, some of whom turn out to be bad shepherds, who do not care for the flock (Ezek. 34:1-10).

In this unit (Zech. 11:4-14), the prophet acts out the role of Yahweh as the over-shepherd of his people and his response to bad under-shepherds, circa 586 BCE. In the next unit (11:15-17), the prophet portrays the "worthless shepherds" of Israel.

In this unit, the symbolic act is in two parts—vv. 4-9 describes a double abandonment (the flock and its leaders have abandoned Yahweh, so Yahweh abandons them to judgment), and vv. 10-14 describes a double annulment (Yahweh annuls his covenant and the brotherhood between Israel and Judah, and the people annul their relationship with Yahweh as their shepherd, paying him out a mere thirty pieces of silver).

The double abandonment echoes the language and imagery of Jeremiah and Ezekiel. In Zech. 11:4, the people are described as "flock doomed for slaughter" *[Jer. 12:3, cf. Jer. 7:32 and 19:6]*. The shepherds described in 11:5 who profit from selling the flock and do not care for the flock are just like the bad shepherds in *[Ezek. 34:2-3]*. As a result of shepherds who do not show pity, Yahweh declares in 11:6, "I will no longer show pity," echoing *[Jer. 13:14]*.

There is a textual issue in v. 7 (and similarly v. 11), which turns on a redivision of the consonantal text of the MT. The MT reads *lākēn ʿăniyēy* (lit. "therefore the afflicted of … "), which is reflected in the NASB and NIV. The awkwardness of this translation suggests that the better approach is to follow the lead of the LXX, which has evidently read the two words as one (*lkn ʿnyy*) and rendered this as "Canaanite." The word "Canaanite" can also be translated "trader" or "merchant" (cf. Zech. 14:21), which is the basis of the translation of the RSV, NEB, NRSV, and ESV. The "merchants of the flock" in Zech. 11:7 and 11:11 are those previously described in v. 5, who sell the flock for profit.

The remainder of v. 8 and v. 9 describes the outworking of the judgment of exile, echoing Jeremiah's description of what happened circa 586 BCE. The flock detested the Yahweh their shepherd, and Yahweh grew weary of the flock *[cf. Jer. 15:6]*. In v. 9 the shepherd abandons the flock who have abandoned him, declaring "I will not be your shepherd. Let the dying die, and the perishing perish," echoing *[Jer. 15:2]*. As a result, those who are left eat one another's flesh *[cf. Jer. 19:9]*.

The second stage of the symbolic act is recorded in vv. 10-14 with a double annulment. It begins with the prophet breaking a staff to annul "my covenant with the peoples." Although some interpret this as some form of universal covenant, the better approach is to take "the peoples" here as a (slightly unusual) reference to the peoples of Israel and Judah (see, e.g., Meyers and Meyers 1993:270–1, cf. Stead 2011:157 for an intertextual argument based on *[Gen. 17:14-16]*). On this basis, the breaking of the second staff in v. 14 is therefore the outworking of the breaking of the first—the annulment of the covenant between Yahweh and the peoples of Israel and Judah also leads to an annulment of the brotherhood between these nations.

In Zech. 11:11-13, the "merchants of the flock" accept Yahweh's annulment of his covenant and annul their relationship with Yahweh as their shepherd, paying him off as though he was worth nothing more than a slave (i.e., thirty pieces of silver). The prophet is commanded to throw the thirty pieces of silver "to the potter … in the house of Yahweh." The significance of this is obscure, since it is not apparent why there should be a potter in the temple, nor what a potter is supposed to do with the thirty pieces of silver. One option is that "potter" (*ywṣr*) is a textual corruption of 'wṣr ("treasury")—cf. Syriac; RSV and NRSV). Other approaches note that *ywṣr* is not limited to those who work with clay and can include those who mold metal (Torrey 1936; Stead 2011:160–2).

The breaking of staffs in this double annulment clearly echoes the imagery of *[Ezek. 37:15-17]*. However, Zech. 11:4-15 is not a repudiation of the promises of restoration in Ezekiel 37 (so most). Rather, Zechariah 11 is retrospective, depicting the historic annulment of the "covenant" and "brotherhood," the restoration of which is depicted in Ezekiel's symbolic act (Meyers and Meyers 1993:301).

11:15-17 Judgment on a Worthless Shepherd

The final unit in Zechariah 11 pivots from past to present. Because a previous generation had rejected Yahweh as their shepherd, the current flock is subject to worthless shepherds. In this symbolic act, the prophet no longer portrays Yahweh as shepherd and instead is to portray a bad shepherd. The description of the foolish shepherd draws largely on Ezekiel's castigation of the bad shepherds in *[Ezek. 34:1-14]*. This unit ends with a glimmer of hope, with a word of judgment pronounced on the worthless shepherd. However, since this deliverance is future, it reinforces the message that the flock is currently subject to bad shepherds.

Zechariah 11 thus ends on a note that circles back to 10:2-3—Yahweh's flock continues to be oppressed by shepherds who do not care for them, and the promises of new leadership, restoration, and salvation held out in Zechariah 9–10 have not yet arrived.

Zechariah 12–14

The final oracle (Zechariah 12–14) explains what will happen on the Day of Yahweh (see 14:1). The refrain "on that day" occurs sixteen times in these chapters, describing the events and impact of that day from a number of different perspectives. The intertextuality of Zechariah 12–14 uses the past to envision the future. The apocalyptic depiction of the final battle draws on Israel's experiences in 586 BCE but with some important twists.

12:1-2 A Cup That Sends the Nations Reeling

That which will occur "on that day" is introduced by allusions to Isaiah 51, to bring to remembrance that Yahweh, *who stretches out the heavens and who lays the foundations of the earth [Isa. 51:13]* and *forms the human spirit* (cf. Isa. 44:2-3) is also the one who promised to take the "cup of staggering" from his people and give it to their tormentors instead *[Isa. 51:22-23]*. Zechariah 12–14 is to be understood in the context of these promises—it will involve a new creation (cf. Zechariah 14), a transforming by the Spirit (12:10) and a reversal for the nations.

12:3-8 A Day When the Nations Gather against Jerusalem

The imagery of Yahweh gathering the nations for war against Jerusalem echoes (or is echoed by) *[Joel 3:1-17 (MT 4:1-17) and Ezekiel 38–19]*. See comments below on Zechariah 14.

In this battle, Yahweh will save his people and defeat the nations. Verses 4–6 redirect the covenant curses of *[Deut. 28:28]* (smiting with panic, madness, and blindness) against the nations, combined with imagery that recalls similar great victories of the past (e.g., causing horse and rider to panic = *[Exod. 14:23-24]*, a flaming torch among the sheaves = *[Judg. 15:1-8]*).

Although there is a differentiation between the "clans of Judah" and the inhabitants of Jerusalem in vv. 5-6, both Jerusalem (12:6) and Judah (12:7) will be saved on the day. Some of the imagery echoes Zechariah 9–11—Yahweh's protection will be a "shield" (cf. Zech. 9:15) and the feeble will be made strengthened (cf. Zech. 10:6).

12:9-14 A Day of Repentance

Although Zech. 12:9 is sometimes treated as an inclusion that concludes the first unit, it is better understood as the beginning of the next unit, providing chronological continuity between the two—on the same day that Yahweh seeks to destroy the nations who have come against Jerusalem (12:9), he will *also* pour [his] Spirit *[Ezek. 39:29]* on the house of David and the inhabitants of Jerusalem (12:10a). This Spirit is "a spirit of grace and supplication" that will lead to weeping *[cf. Jer. 31:9]*. The trigger for this outpouring is described in Zech. 12:10b with three verbs—to look, to pierce, and to mourn—each of which raises exegetical questions: who are they looking at, who was pierced, and for whom do they mourn?

- "Look"—many scholars (e.g., Mitchell 1912:334-5) propose that "they will look *to me*" should be amended to "they will look *at him*" to bring this into conformity with the third person "mourn *for him*" later in the verse, so as to avoid the implication that the people have pierced Yahweh. However, there is no textual warrant for this, and the overall message of this section, which describes national mourning, presupposes a "looking to" Yahweh, which would be lost if this verse was amended.

- "Pierce"—the second clause is introduced with a direct object marker and relative pronoun, which is curious, because the prior verb already has an object ("they will look *to me*"). Meyer and Meyers (1993:337) argue that this construction functions as a demonstrative and can be translated "they will look to me *concerning* the one they have pierced." Alternatively, it could be that the verb *nbṭ* (look) has double objects, with *ʾel* denoting whom they *look to*, and *ʾēt ʾăšer* denoting what they *look at*—"they will look *to me*, looking *at* the one they have pierced ...."

- "Mourn"—the identity of the pierced one is not explained. However, there are two clues in the following verses. Firstly, the death of the pierced one leads to grief like that of parents over the loss of their only child and heir *[cf. Jer. 6:26]*, except that here the grief extends to the whole nation, clan by clan (see 12:12-14). The whole nation mourns because their future hopes have (seemingly) been extinguished by this death. Secondly, the reference to weeping in the plain of Megiddo recalls the death of King Josiah *[2 Chron. 35:20-24, cf. 2 Kgs 23:29-30]* (contra Redditt 1995:133, that this refers to a ritual mourning for a storm God called Hadad-rimmon). The death of this unidentified figure will be another national catastrophe, as terrible as the day that good King Josiah died. These two clues hint that the one who has been pierced is a Davidic King. This also explains why the *House of* David is prominent in Zechariah 12, yet there is no reference to the Davidic King himself.

In Zech. 12:12-14, the "whole land" mourns, particularized as the house of David and other named family groups. This is presumably the same as "the house of David and the inhabitants of Jerusalem" (12:10, cf. 13:1). Those upon whom Yahweh has poured out his Spirit respond in weeping and supplication, and it is for the same group that a "fountain of cleansing" is opened (13:1).

13:1 A Day of Cleansing

Although there may be overtones from Jer. 2:13 ("fountain of living water"), Ezekiel 36 provides the dominant imagery for this verse. In *[Ezek. 36:25-26]*, Yahweh promises to sprinkle clean water to cleanse the people from impurity and idolatry, and to put a new Spirit in them. The fountain in Zech. 13:1 depicts this. The word for impurity in Zech. 13:1, which can also mean menstrual uncleanness, also occurs in *[Ezek. 36:17]* where is used metaphorically of idolatry. The connotation of idolatry provides the link to the next unit.

13:2-6 A Day When Idolatry and False Prophecy Will Be Banished from the Land

It is convenient to treat 13:2-3 and 4-6 as a single unit, because of the interrelationship between idolatry and false prophecy (see comments above on Zech. 10:1-2). On the day on which Yahweh opens a fountain to cleanse his people (cf. 13:1), he will also remove the idols and their promoters. The idols will be removed so completely that they will no longer be remembered *[Hos. 2:16-17 (MT 18–19)]*.

Yahweh will also remove "the prophets" and "spirit of uncleanness." The interpretation of these two phrases is connected. Removing "the prophets" does not signal the "end of prophecy" *per se*, but the end of *false* prophecy. This is clear from what these "prophets" do—they "tell lies in Yahweh's name" (13:3) and "deceive" (13:4). In light of this, the "spirit of uncleanness" is best taken as a reference to the spirits who inspire false prophecy, such as the "lying spirit" of 1 Kgs 22:22-23. As such, this verse describes the complete removal of both the human agents and the evil spiritual forces at work in false prophecy.

As noted above, the condemnation for lying in Yahweh's name *[Jer. 14:14]* also has overtones from *[Deut. 21:18-21]* (a father and mother putting to death a rebellious son), *[Deut. 13:6-10]* (the death penalty for leading others into apostasy), and/or *[Deut. 18:20-22]* (the prophet who speaks presumptuously in Yahweh's name).

For this reason, the false prophet will "be ashamed of his prophetic vision" *[cf. Mic. 3:7]* and seek to conceal his identity in three ways. Firstly, he will "not put on a prophet's garment of hair in order to deceive," which alludes to both Elijah's distinctive hairy garment *[2 Kgs 1:8, 2:13]* and the "hairy deception" in *[Gen. 27:11-16, cf. Gen. 25:25]*. Secondly, he will claim "I am not a prophet," inverting *[Amos 7:14]*. Thirdly, he will dismiss the wounds on his body (self-inflicted cultic cutting *[see 1 Kgs 18:28, Deut. 14:1, Jer. 16:6, and Jer. 47:5]*) as wounds from friends.

13:7-9 A Day of the Sword—Refining Judgment on the Land

The final unit in ch. 13 stands apart from that which precedes it. This "sword oracle" draws heavily on *[Ezekiel 21]*, which describes a sword of judgment that Yahweh is about to bring on his people, by sending the king of Babylon against them (Ezek. 21:3). The climax of the sword's destructive work is seen in the death of the Davidic King (Ezek. 21:10, cf. 21:13 and 21:26). Ezekiel 21 pointed to the events of 586 BCE, but Zechariah 13 repurposes this to envision a future sword of judgment, which will strike "my shepherd, the man who is close to me." These two phrases have unmistakable royal overtones—see esp. *[Ezek. 34:23]* ("my shepherd") and "he will come close to me" *[Jer. 30:21]*. Thus when Yahweh calls this sword to "awaken," he is hastening a sword against his anointed king.

Zech. 13:7b-8 describes the immediate consequences of the death— the sword will "strike the shepherd, and the sheep will be scattered" *[1 Kgs 22:17]*. This judgment will be terrible in its consequences—even the "little ones" will be caught up in this judgment, and two-thirds of the populace "will be struck down and perish" *[Ezek. 5:11-12]*. These verses describe a coming judgment on the nation that will be as terrible as the destruction wrought by the Babylonian armies in 586 BCE. Like that earlier judgment, however, there will also be a remnant who survive and be refined by the process *[Isa. 1:25-28]*. According to 13:9, "They will call on my name and I will answer them; I will say, 'They are my people,' and they will say, 'Yahweh is our God'" *[cf. Zech. 10:6b+9a; Hos. 2:21-23 [MT 23–25].*

14:1-5 A Day … of Distress and Battle

Zech. 14:1 begins with an announcement that Yahweh's Day is coming. As elsewhere, this "Day of Yahweh" will be both a day of judgment and a day of salvation (see, e.g., Zeph. 1:14-18, Joel 2:1-2). The day begins darkly for Jerusalem, with the city under attack. This vision of the Day of Yahweh draws on the historical experiences of Jerusalem in 586 BCE. What Babylon did in the past becomes the paradigm for what the nations will do when they gather against Jerusalem *[Ezek. 38:1-6, 16; Joel 3:2 [4:2], cf. Zech. 12:1].* The nations will seize the spoil *[Ezek. 38:12-13].* As in *[Isa. 13:16]*, houses will be plundered and the women raped. It will begin as it did in 597 BCE, with half the city taken into exile. But then comes the twist. In 586 BCE, the "rest of the people in the city" were taken into exile [**2 Kgs 25:11**]. But here, the "rest of the people shall **not** be cut off from the city." This is because Yahweh will go out and fight against the nations (14:3). As in *[Ezek. 38:19-22]*, this will include a topographic rearrangement.

Unlike 586 BCE, when the people tried to flee from Jerusalem but were captured on the plains (2 Kgs 25:4-6), Yahweh will provide a mountain valley as an escape route for his people, by splitting the Mount of Olives in two, "to Azal." The reference to Azal is uncertain, but it may refer to a location at the end of the Azal Valley (Nahal Azal in modern Israel), which is to the south of the Mount of Olives. If this is the case, then "Azal" is not the direction to which the people flee, but rather marks the extent to which the Mount of Olives has shifted south. There are two allusions that highlight the significance of the Mount of Olives. Translating literally, the final clause tells us that the Mount of Olives is "in the face of Jerusalem, from the east." The only prior instances of the phrase "in the face of Jerusalem" are in 1 Kgs 11:7 and 2 Kgs 23:13, with reference to the location of idolatrous shrines that Solomon has set up for his wives on the Mount of Olives. Translating "in the face of" colloquially, we might say that idolatry was going on "right under the nose of" Jerusalem. The second allusion is in the (semi-redundant) information that the Mount of Olives is "east of Jerusalem." This geographic marker is a reminder that when the Yahweh's glory had departed from Jerusalem, it had stopped above the mountain to the "east of the city"

[Ezek. 11:23], and that Yahweh's return to Jerusalem would be from the same direction *[Ezek. 43:2]*. In Zech. 14:4, Yahweh returns as promised via the Mount of Olives and in the process destroys that place of idolatry.

14:6-7 A Day of New Creation

Various amendments have been proposed to resolve the apparent contradiction between "there will be no light" (14:6) and "there will be light" (14:7). However, rather than amend the MT, these verses can be understood as describing a sequence of events—no light, followed by light. That is, the Day of Yahweh will initially manifest as a day without light *[Isa. 13:9-10, cf. Zeph. 1:14-15; Amos 5:18; Joel 2:1-2]*. But this day of darkness will give way to a day of perpetual light, as promised in *[Isa. 60:19-20]*.

14:8-12 A Restored Land

Verses 8–11 describe a series of geographical and geological transformations that will occur on the Day of Yahweh.

Living waters will flow out from the temple in Jerusalem (14:8) to bring fecundity to the land *[Ezek. 47:8 and Joel 3:18 (MT 4:18)]*. What had once been desert and arid plains will become fertile and productive.

Yahweh himself will be king over all the land (14:9). The earlier interest in the Davidic King (cf. Zech. 9:9) is no longer relevant, because Yahweh himself is on the throne. The "shema" of ancient Israel—"Hear, O Israel: Yahweh our God, Yahweh is one" *[Deut. 6:4]*—is the unchallenged reality.

Zech. 14:10-11 describe topological rearrangements that highlight the security and significance of Jerusalem. The region *from Geba to Rimmon* (i.e., the whole territory of Judah) will become a flat plain, *like the Arabah*, while Jerusalem will be raised up to have the exalted place *[Isa. 2:2]*. The gates mentioned in this verse are part of the city walls that marked out the perimeter of Jerusalem *[Jer. 31:38-40]*.

However, we do not (yet) see the pilgrimage of the nations to the exalted Jerusalem described in Isaiah 2. Instead, the nations who gathered to fight against Jerusalem are struck with plagues (14:12), like Egypt in the days of the Exodus and the enemies in *[Isa. 66:24]*. This description of the enemy nations in the land both rounds out the third section and provides a transition in the final section, from Zech. 14:13-21.

14:13-21 A Day of Transformation

14:13-15 continues the theme of v. 12. Yahweh will strike the nations with great panic *[Deut. 7:23]*. In confusion, the enemy nations will attack each other *[Ezek. 38:21]*. The plague that Yahweh sent against the nations will also strike the animals in their camps (14:15, cf. *[Exod. 9:3-4]*).

While the nations are falling apart, Judah and Jerusalem will come together, and together they will plunder the nations (14:14). Those who had formerly been plundered by the nations (cf. 14:1-2) will become the plunderers *[Zech. 2:9]*.

However, the goal of the overthrow of the nations is not obliteration, but to bring the nations into submission to Yahweh. In 14:16, some of the warriors have become worshippers. The final fate of nations is pilgrimage to Jerusalem, echoing *[Zech. 8:20-23, cf. Isa. 2:1-4||Mic. 4:1-4 and Isa. 60:5-21]*. The imagery in this unit also has several distinct points of correspondence with *[Isa. 66:18-24]*.

However, unlike these other passages, the survivors from the nations come to celebrate the Feast of Tabernacles. This annual festival occurred at the end of the agricultural year, after the ingathering of the harvest, in praise of Yahweh's material blessing on the people. The reason why this harvest festival is singled out in particular might be related to the fate of those who do not worship—according to vv. 17-19, they will suffer drought and plagues (and hence no harvest), whereas those who worship Yahweh will be blessed with a harvest for which they come to give thanks.

This unit ends with an image of a transformed Jerusalem. In 14:20-21, Jerusalem has become one massive sanctuary—so much so, that even the most common of objects will be sacred. The phrase that was once written on the high priest's turban—"Holy to Yahweh" *[Exod. 28:36]*—will now be written on objects as common as the bells on horses, and ordinary cooking pots will be like the sacred bowls before the altar. Holiness will not be limited to the specially consecrated items in the temple. All of Jerusalem will be a "holy" zone. A further sign of the purity of the city is that "there will no longer be a Canaanite (that is, a merchant) in the house of Yahweh of hosts."

Appendix

Figure 5.11 Textual variances between MT and LXX

Zechariah 9–14—Textual variances between MT and LXX			
Verse	**MT text**	**MT translation**	**LXX translation**	**LXX vorlage**
9:1	mənûḥâ	resting place	sacrifice	minḥâ
9:10	mîyām	from sea	the waters	mayim
9:12	ngd	announce	captivity	gwr
9:13	śym	place	grope	mšš
10:1	ḥăzîzîm	storm clouds	visions	ḥzh
10:4	yātēd	tent peg	he arranged	yʿd
10:4	milḥāmâ	battle-(bow)	in anger	b + ḥēmâ
10:12	hlk	walk	boast, praise	hll
11:7,11	kēn ʿănîyēy	so the afflicted	Canannites	knʿny
11:7,14	ḥōbəlîm	union	cord	ḥebel
11:7	ʾeḥād	one	other	ʾaḥēr
11:13	yôṣēr	potter	smelting furnace	???
11:14	ʾaḥawâ	brotherhood	possession	ʾăḥuzzâ
11:16	hannaʿar	the young	the wandering	ʿwr
11:16	habbrîʾâ	the fat ones	the chosen	brr
12:3	maʿamāsâ	heavy	trodden	mrmsh
12:5	ʾamṣâ	strengthen	find	mṣʾ
12:10	dāqārû	pierce	mocked	rqd
12:11	hădad-rimmôn	Hadad-Rimmon	pomegranate	rimmôn
12:11	məgiddôn	Megiddo	cut down	gdʿ
13:1	māqôr	fountain	place	mqwm
13:3	ûdəqāruhû	pierce him	bind his feet	ʿqd
13:7	haṣṣōʿărîm	the little ones	the shepherds	hrʿym
14:1	nws	flee	be blocked up	stm
14:5	ngʿ	touch	be joined to	???
14:5	nws	flee x2	be blocked up	stm
14:5	mippnēy	in the face	in the day	bymy
14:6	yāqār	cold	and cold	w + qōr

6

Malachi

6.1 Author

The book of Malachi is the last of the three postexilic prophets. The Hebrew word in Mal. 1:1, which is rendered in English as "Malachi," means "my messenger" or "my angel." There is some debate as to whether Malachi is a personal name or a functional description. Smith argues that "my messenger" is a "very unlikely appellation for a parent to bestow on a child," and that the name "Malachi" was attached to the book by an editor under the influence of Mal. 3:1 (1912:9). (See similarly Petersen 1995:165, Weyde 2000:62–3.) This argument is bolstered by the LXX, which renders the word as "his messenger/angel," and the Targum of Jonathan, which adds to Mal. 1:1 "his name is Ezra the scribe." Calvin countenanced the possibility that the book was written by Ezra, and Malachi is a pseudonym (1849:459).

However, other scholars are not persuaded that "Malachi" is inappropriate as a proper name with some suggesting that it may be a name that the prophet took on when he commenced his ministry (see Hill 1998:15–18 for details). The trend in more recent scholarship is to treat Malachi as a proper name (see, e.g., Glazier-MacDonald 1987:28–9, Verhoef 1987:155–6, Hill 1998:15–18, Snyman 2015:25–7).

There are no other scriptural references to a prophet named Malachi, so all that is known about the prophetic ministry of Malachi is that which can be inferred from the book. The lack of personal information puts the emphasis on his role as "Yahweh's messenger" to speak the word of Yahweh to his generation.

6.2 Date

The reference to a governor (*peḥâ*) in Mal. 1:8 locates the book in the Persian period or later (cf. Hag. 1:1; Ezra 8:36; Neh. 2:7; Esth. 3:12), and the call to shut the doors to the altar in Mal. 1:10 implies that the temple has been rebuilt (and cf. Mal. 3:1 and 3:10). Hence the book must be dated after the completion of the temple in 515 BCE (cf. Ezra 6:15). The reference to the destruction of Edom in Mal. 1:2-4, about which there are historical uncertainties but which is presumed to predate 515 BCE, gives no further assistance in dating.

There is a striking difference in tone between Haggai and Zechariah 1–8 on the one hand and Malachi on the other. In the former, there is an affirmation of the leadership of Zerubbabel (governor) and Joshua (High Priest), and the people of God are encouraged to expect the imminent fulfillment of God's promises to restore Jerusalem. In contrast, Malachi is deeply critical of the priests of its day, the governor plays no significant role, and the people are both challenged and confronted because they have become discouraged and disillusioned by the wait for God to keep his promise (see further Verhoef 1987:157). This suggests that the book of Malachi is addressed to a situation a generation or more removed from the context of Haggai and Zechariah 1–8.

There are significant thematic similarities between Malachi and Ezra-Nehemiah, which are shown in the following table.

Mixed marriages	Mal. 2:10-16	Ezra 9:1-15; 10:1-17; Neh. 13:23-28
Tithing	Mal. 3:7b-10	Neh. 13:10-12
Social injustice	Mal. 3:5	Neh. 5:1-13; 13:15-22
Corrupt priesthood	Mal. 1:6-2:9	Neh. 13:7-9, 28-31

These overlapping issues suggest ministries at a broadly similar stage in history. However, there are several factors that suggest that Malachi's ministry probably preceded Nehemiah. Firstly, the tribute provided to the governor in Mal. 1:8 points to a situation prior to Nehemiah (cf. Neh. 5:14-18). Secondly, the rhetoric of Mal. 2:10-12 suggests that the people were unaware that "marrying the daughter of a foreign God" profaned the covenant, which would be unlikely if Malachi came after Nehemiah. Thirdly, it is unlikely that Malachi's ministry directly overlapped with either Ezra or Nehemiah, since this is not referred to in either book.

On the basis of a typological analysis of its linguistic affinities with Haggai and Zechariah 1–8, Hill argues that Malachi was composed between 515 and 458 BCE with a likely date between 500 and 475 BCE (1983, cf. 1998:80–4, 395–401). However, there are polarized views on the viability of dating Hebrew texts on this basis—compare Polzin (1976), Hurvitz (2000), Young, Rezetko, and Ehrensvärd (2008), and Shin (2016).

For much of the twentieth century, scholarship on Malachi was influenced by the Graf-Wellhausen Documentary Hypothesis: that the Pentateuch was composed of **J**ahwist (=Yahwist), **E**lohist, **D**euteronomist, and **P**riestly Codes (JEDP). According to Wellhausen, D was composed circa 620 BCE, during the reign of King Josiah, and P reflects later (i.e., postexilic) temple-centric and priestly concerns. Wellhausen argued that the Priestly Code did not become part of the Pentateuch until 444 BCE, in association with Ezra's ministry (1957:405, 496). According to Wellhausen, one of the key features of P is a sharp distinction between the sons of Aaron and the Levites (1957:497). On the basis of this hypothesis, it has been commonly argued that since Malachi does not make a distinction between Priests and Levites and otherwise reflects the D documentary tradition, therefore Malachi must predate P (see, e.g., Elliger and Weiser 1963:178).

However, the analysis of O'Brien (1990) has demonstrated that, while "priests" and "sons of Levi" are synonymous in Malachi, Malachi does not consistently reflect D tradition and has some vocabulary in common with P and is not entirely dependent on either tradition. O'Brien argues that the author of Malachi may have had access to an already integrated form of both D and P (or perhaps even the Pentateuch in its final form).

Although it is not possible to speak of a consensus, the majority of scholars date Malachi in the first half of the fifth century BCE (so, e.g., Elliger, Wellhausen, Eisfeldt, Ackroyd, Hill, Merrill, Berquist, Petersen—see Hill 1998:393–5 for details). Some scholars suggest a more precise date range—for example, Glazier-MacDonald (1987:14–18)—470–450 BCE, Reventlow (1993:130), and Snyman (2015:2)—460–450 BCE, cf. Verhoef (1987:158), who dates Malachi between the first and second governorships of Nehemiah (*c*. 433 BCE).

6.3 Text

The MT of Malachi has no *ketiv*/*qere*. The most significant textual issues relate to Mal. 2:15-16, where it seems most versions have struggled to wrestle meaning from an obscure text (Fuller 1991).

Text-critical issues on these verses, and on Mal. 2:3 and Mal. 2:12, are discussed in §6.8.

Fragments of Malachi are found in 4QXII[a] (2:10-3:24), 4QXII[c] (3:7), 4QCommMal. (3:16-18). By comparison with the very small number of variants for Haggai and Zechariah, there are proportionately more variations between the MT and 4QXII[a] (Ego et al. 2005:191–5). The reading in 4QXIIa Mal. 2:12 (ʿd instead of ʿr) supports the LXX against the MT.

The LXX of Malachi exhibits similar patterns as already noted in relation to Haggai and Zechariah, including periphrastic renditions (e.g., LXX Mal. 1:7 has an extra clause at the end), interpretive expansions (e.g., Mal. 3:5 "swear falsely" becomes "swear falsely in my name"), and misreading the Hebrew—for example, Mal. 2:15, reading ʾḥr ("another") instead of ʾeḥād ("one").

Mal. 4:1-6 in the Vulgate and English versions corresponds to Mal. 3:19-24 in the MT and LXX with a different sequence for the final three verses in the LXX.

6.4 Genre and Composition

Malachi consists of oracular prose even if at times it reflects elements of a poetic style (see Hill 1998:23-26; contra Glazier-MacDonald 1987a:6).

Like Zech. 9:1 and 12:1, Malachi 1 begins with the phrase maśśā' dəbar-YHWH ("Oracle, word of Yahweh"), which are the only three instances of this phrase. (See §5.2 on maśśā' as a genre tag.)

Petersen (1995:165) argues for a tight connection between Zechariah 9–11, Zechariah 12–14, and Malachi, and in particular that Malachi is the "third in a series of deuteroprophetic collections," in which these three oracles follow the typical sequence found in other prophetic works—oracles against nations (Zechariah 9–11), oracles against Israel (Zechariah 12–14), and oracles on behalf of Israel (Malachi). Others have argued that the maśśā' superscriptions were added to link these units in the process of the formation of the Book of the Twelve (Nogalski 1993b:187–9).

However, the three maśśā' superscriptions differ from each other in both form and function (see Childs 1979:491–2, Floyd 2002:415–16). Moreover, as Petersen acknowledges, "the third 'oracle' is decidedly different from the foregoing ones ... Instead of persistent eschatological emphasis, immediate verbal encounter between the deity and the other parties characterises the final 'oracle'" (1995:29). On this basis, it is best to approach Malachi as a stand-alone prophetic word, independent of any presumed connection with Zechariah 9–14.

Figure 6.1 The rîb pattern in Malachi

The rîb pattern in Malachi (O'Brien 1990)

I)   Prologue: (1:2–5)
II)   Accusations
  A)   First Accusation (1:6—2:9a)
    1) Preliminaries (1:6a)
    2) Interrogation (1:6b)
    3) Indictment (1:7–10a)
    4) Declaration of guilt (1:10b–14)
    5) Ultimatum/Punishment (2:1–9)
  B)   B. Second Accusation (2:10–16)
    1) Preliminaries (2:10a)
    2) Interrogation (2:10b)
    3) Indictment (2:11)
    4) Declaration of guilt (2:12)
    5) Further indictment (2:13–14)
    6) Ultimatum/Warning (2:15–16)
  C)   Third Accusation (2:17—3:5)
    1) Indictment (2:17)
    2) Ultimatum/Promise (3:1–5)
  D)   Fourth Accusation (3:6–12)
    1) Preliminaries (3:6)
    2) Indictment (3:7a)
    3) Ultimatum/Promise (3:7b)
    4) Indictment (3:8–9)
    5) Promise (3:10–12)
  E)   Fifth Accusation (3:13–21)
    1) Indictment (3:13–15)
    2) Historical Account (3:16–18)
    3) Ultimatum/Promise (3:19–21)
III) Final Admonition (3:22 [4:4])
IV)   Final Ultimatum (3:23–24 [4:5-6])

O'Brien argues that Malachi follows the genre of the covenant lawsuit (*rîb*). O'Brien builds on the work of Harvey (1967:66), who identified an incomplete *rîb* form in Mal. 1:6–2:9.

O'Brien applied Harvey's insight to the book as a whole: "The entire Book of Malachi, indeed, employs the form of the covenant lawsuit. The elements that Harvey traces in 1:6-2:9 resound throughout the book" (1990:63). The *rîb* pattern in Malachi identified by O'Brien is shown in Figure 6.1.

While O'Brien's approach helpfully underscores the covenantal basis of the accusations raised, the correspondences with *rîb* form are not exact. It is unlikely that Malachi was consciously conforming to a particular treaty/lawsuit structure, given the variations in the five accusations identified in O'Brien's structure. O'Brien's attempts to conform Malachi to the *rîb* structure are at some points forced (see Hill 1998:32–3, cf. Floyd 2000:564–6).

Some argue that Malachi has a complex redactional history. For example, Redditt argues a redactor has combined

> two written collections of materials from the same prophet. The first collection (1:6–2:9; 2:11[?]13-16) castigated the priests; the second (1:2-5; 2:10,12; 2:17-3:1a + 3:5; 3:6-7; 3:8-12; and possibly 3:13-15) condemned the laity. The redactor provided the superscription (1:1) and most of chap. 3, specifically 3:1b-4,13-21 (reapplying 3:13-15,18). Either he or the redactor of the Book of the Twelve added 3:22-24 (Engl. 4:4-6).
>
> (1994:249)

In contrast, Bosshard and Kratz (1990) argue for three layers—a foundational layer consisting 1:2-5 (probably), 1:6-2:9, 2:13-16, 3:6-12; a second layer consisting of 2:17-3:5 and 3:13-4:3 [MT 3:21]; and a final redaction that added 1:1, 1:14a, 2:10-12, and 4:4-6 [MT 3:22-24].

However, as Nogalski (2011:998–9) notes, the idea of interpolations or redactional layers has not taken hold in Malachi scholarship because "Malachi's unity and diversity is better explained as editorial compilation, arrangement, and adaptation of source material than through models of gradual accretion."

6.5 Structure

Since the pivotal work of Pfeiffer (1959), the book of Malachi has been commonly recognized to consist of six "disputation speeches," each consisting of an opening statement, followed by a defense in the form of a question and a response based on the opening statement.

My analysis of the structure shown in Figure 6.2, which is a variation on Pfeiffer, takes each speech to be structured around a reported question of the people, which is introduced with the formula, "But you say 'How/why … '" (*wa ʾamartem* + the interrogative *mâ*).

In each disputation, the reported question of the people is prompted by a statement, rhetorical question, or accusation from Yahweh or his prophet. Yahweh is the speaker in the first two and last two disputations. The prophet is the speaker in the middle two.

Malachi 2:10-16 is a variation on the pattern of the other speeches. The people are accused of two forms of marital unfaithfulness—marrying "daughters of a foreign god" and divorce. The structure of the first issue (foreign wives) departs from the pattern described above, in that it is introduced by a triplex of rhetorical questions ("Have we not all one Father? Has not one God created us? Why then are we faithless to one another, profaning the covenant of our fathers?"). The second issue (divorce) reverts to the pattern, in that it is introduced by a statement and reported question, "**But you say**, 'Why does he not [*accept our offerings*]?'" (2:14).

There are parallels between the second and fifth disputations. Both have double questions and concern the topic of offerings. The second disputation is addressed to the priests, whereas the fifth disputation is addressed to all the people.

There are also parallels between the fourth and sixth disputations. Both accuse the people of speaking words against Yahweh, questioning the justice of God. Both passages address this matter with reference to the future coming of Yahweh as judge, and one who will prepare his way. The fourth disputation is focused on the purification of the priests before a day of judgment, whereas the sixth disputation is focused on the judgment of the wicked and the preservation of the righteous on the day of judgment.

There is a general consensus among scholars about the point of demarcation between the six speeches, except for a diversity of views about whether Mal. 3:6 is the conclusion to the fourth disputation, the beginning of the fifth, or a bridge verse that links the fourth and fifth units.

The short narrative in Mal. 3:16 that describes the response of those who feared the Lord is a departure from the disputational style of the book (Nogalski 1993b: 185). The conclusion in 4:4-6 (MT 3:22-24) is also a departure from the disputational style elsewhere. The significance of these variations will be discussed below.

Figure 6.2 The structure of Malachi

	Type	Prompt	Reported question	Response
1:1-5	Statement (Yahweh)	2 "I have loved you" says Yahweh	**But you say**, "How have you loved us?"	"I have loved Jacob 3 and I have hated Esau"
1:6-2:9	Rhetorical Question (Yahweh)	6 A son honours his father, and a servant his master. If then I am a father, where is my honour? And if I am a master, where is my fear? says Yahweh of hosts to you, O priests, who despise my name.	**But you say**, "How have we despised your name?" 7 By offering polluted food upon my altar. **But you say**, "How have we polluted you?"	By saying that Yahweh's table may be despised.
2:10-16	Rhetorical Questions		triplex of rhetorical questions *[see below]*	
	Statement (Prophet)	13 Yahweh … no longer accepts your offerings	14 **But you say**, 'Why does he not?'	Because Yahweh is a witness between you and the wife of your youth, to whom you have been faithless
2:17-3:6	Accusation (Prophet)	17 You have wearied Yahweh with your words.	**But you say**, "How have we wearied him?"	By saying, "Everyone who does evil is good…"
3:7-12	Accusation (Yahweh)	7 From the days of your fathers you have turned aside from my statutes and have not kept them. Return to me, and I will return to you, says the Yahweh of hosts.	**But you say**, 'How shall we return?' 8 Will man rob God? Yet you are robbing me. **But you say**, 'How have we robbed you?'	9 In your tithes and offerings …. You are robbing me—the whole nation of you!
3:13-4:6	Accusation (Yahweh)	13 "Your words have been hard against me," says Yahweh.	**But you say**, 'How have we spoken against you?'	14 You have said "It is vain to serve Yahweh"

What is the literary arrangement of the six units? According to Baldwin (1972:214), the subjects "follow one another apparently haphazardly." In contrast, Assis (2010:363–4) discerns an overarching structure, whereby the

> book is divided into two parts: the first deals with the relationship between Israel and the nations, the second with the question of injustice in God's judgment. Each of these subjects is made up of three prophetic units. In each part, the first oracle and the third are closely interrelated. In both parts the middle oracle (the second and the fifth) is a cultic application of the relevant matter.

The structure proposed by Assis is shown in Figure 6.3.

Although not convinced by all aspects of Assis's argument or his unit demarcation at 1:9, there is merit in the overall structure proposed. The first set of three units is bound together by the notion of covenant (covenantal election [1:2-5], covenant with Levi [1:6-2:9], profaning the covenant of our fathers [2:10-16]). The second set of three units is linked by the issue of "cause and effect theology."

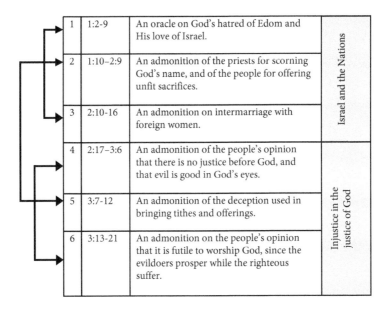

Figure 6.3 The structure of Malachi (Assis)

6.6 The Covenant-Centric Intertextuality of Malachi

There have been a number of significant investigations into Malachi's reuse of biblical texts traditions, including Utzschneider (1989), Berry (1996), and Weyde (2000).

A recent analysis by Gibson (2016) argues that inner-biblical allusions to biblical covenants shapes Malachi's entire message. It is often observed that the concept of covenant is central to Malachi's message (e.g., Baldwin 1972:216; Verhoef 1987:180; Redditt 1995:156; Hill 1998:43), but Gibson goes further and identifies allusions to the patriarchal covenant, the covenant with Levi, the marriage covenant, the mosaic covenant, the new covenant and covenant renewal. His conclusions (many of which are reflected in the analysis below) are summarized in the following table.

	Covenant	Key inner-biblical allusions
1:1-5	Patriarchal	Yahweh's covenant fidelity is seen in his electing and enduring love for Israel, which is reinforced by allusions to the Jacob-Esau tradition [**Genesis 25–36**], unique word/root combinations with various prophetic texts concerning Edom and Israel [**esp. Ezekiel 35–36**; **Isa. 34.5-15; Joel 3:19-20 (MT 4:19-20)**] and Deuteronomic resonances.
1:6–2:9	Levitical	Despite their special status due to the covenant with Levi [**Num. 25:10-13; Deut. 33:8-11; Exod. 32.25-29**], the priests have failed to honor Yahweh's name by obedience to the sacrificial laws [**Lev. 22:17-25; Deut. 15:21**], which leads to a "command" against them in the form of the Deuteronomic curse [**Deut. 28:15-20,59**] and an inversion of the Priestly Blessing [**Num. 6:23-27**].
2:10-16	Marital (2:13-16)	These verses allude to the marriage of the first human pair [**Gen. 2:23-24**] and the divorce laws in [**Deut. 24:1-4**]. Mal. 2:15-16 neither contradicts nor supersedes the Mosaic law on divorce.
2:17-3:6	New Covenant	The messenger of Yahweh alludes to [**Exod. 23:20**] and recalls exodus imagery. This is combined with an allusion to [**Isa. 40:3**], which has connotations of a *new* exodus. Before this comes, the people will face the terror of the Day of Yahweh [**Joel 2:11**].

	Covenant	Key inner-biblical allusions
3:7-12	Mosaic	The call to repentance echoes **[Zech. 1:2-6]**. While Mal. 3:7-9 actualizes the Deuteronomic curse **[Deut. 28; 30:1-3, 9-10]**, some of the vocabulary used in his offer to bless, upon condition of repentance, demonstrates a reversal of the curse **[Deut. 30:1-3, 9-10]** and the inversion of the flood narrative **[Gen. 7:11, 8:2]**.
3:13-4:3	Covenant renewal	Texts that previously declared all Israel to be Yahweh's special possession **[Exod. 19:5; Deut. 7:6, 14:2, 26:18]** are reapplied to a smaller group—those who fear Yahweh.

6.7 Overview of Malachi—Key Issues

Key intertexts are marked with []—see §2.5 and §6.6.

[I] Malachi 1:1-5

The first disputation is the shortest of the six, but it is fundamental to the rest. Notwithstanding the fact that the word "covenant" is not used, it establishes the covenantal basis on which the other disputations depend.

It is addressed "to Israel" at a time when Israel has ceased to exist as a nation. This has both retrospective and prospective functions. The title "Israel" points back to the nation's beginnings, when Jacob was renamed Israel (which is picked up in 1:2-5). And the title operates prospectively, by reminding the small remnant of Judah to whom the book is addressed that they are in fact the true inheritors of Yahweh's ancient covenant with "Israel."

The word used here to describe Yahweh's "love" (*'hb*) for Israel points back to the foundational expression of God's covenant love in choosing Israel as a nation—for example, Deut. 7:7-8 "Yahweh **chose** (*bḥr*) you because he **loves** (*'hb*) you and is keeping his oath to the forefathers" (cf. Deut. 4:37, 10:15, and 23:5[6]; Gibson 2016:48).

Verses 2–3 argue that Yahweh's love for Israel is demonstrated by the differing treatments of Jacob and Esau—"I have loved Jacob but Esau I have hated," alluding to *[Genesis 25–36]*. Modern readers struggle with this for two reasons. Firstly, they recoil from the statement "Esau I have hated." It is important to recognize that the Hebrew word for "hate" (*śānē'*) has a different semantic range than the English word (cf. Gen. 39:30-31, 2 Sam. 19:6, Exod. 20:5-6). In this context, where "loving Jacob" means choosing to be in covenant with him, "hating Esau" means not choosing him (Assis 2009:110–11). The second reason why modern readers struggle is because of the apparently unfair treatment of Esau. Some commentators shift the focus from the individuals (Jacob and Esau) to their respective nations (Israel and Edom) and explain the ongoing judgment on Edom described in Mal. 1:5 as an appropriate response to Edom's mistreatment of Israel (cf. Redditt 2000).

However, while it is certainly true that Edomites are elsewhere condemned for their violence, profiteering and complicity in the destruction of Jerusalem (e.g., Obadiah 10–15) to make this the point of Mal. 1:2-5 is textually the wrong way around. The reason why Esau is not loved/chosen is *not* because Yahweh has anticipated the future bad behavior of Edom. Rather, the fact that Edom will be destroyed and will *not* return and rebuild is the outworking of Esau not being chosen *[cf. Ezek. 35:10; 36:5; Isa. 34.5-15; Joel 3:19-20 (MT 4:19-20)]*, whereas Israel—who have also sinned—have returned and rebuilt, because they are "loved."

Mal. 1:1-5 argues that Yahweh's electing love for Israel continues to be demonstrated by the respective fortunes of Edom and Israel.

[II] Malachi 1:6-2:9

The second disputation consists of two sections, each addressed to "the priests" (1:6; 2:1). Here, as elsewhere in Malachi, the Levitical priesthood is an undifferentiated whole (O'Brien 1990:146–7; see Petersen 1995:190–3 for the counter view). The priests are "despising" Yahweh by offering blemished sacrifices. As a result, their offerings are unacceptable and the offeror is under a curse. Instead of discharging the responsibilities of the covenant with Levi, they had corrupted the covenant and led many people astray.

The priests "despise" (=treat as worthless; give no weight to) Yahweh's name, like Esau who "despised his birthright" *[Gen. 25:34]*. Rather than treating Yahweh lightly, they should have "honoured" (=give due weight to) him, as Israel's father and "Lord" (ʾādôn). Instead, they have despised Yahweh by offering blind, lame, and diseased animals (1:9), when only sacrifices without blemish were acceptable to the Lord *[Lev. 22:17-25; Deut. 15:21]*. The invitation to seek God's favor (1:9) is sarcastic, because in reality these sacrifices would not even find favor with the governor, much less Yahweh (Glazier-McDonald 1987:51).

Yahweh declares their sacrifices to be **offensive** ("I have no pleasure in you"), **unacceptable** ("I will not accept an offering from your hand"), **useless** ("fire on my altar in vain"), and **defiling** ("you profane it"). Such sacrifices bring a curse on the offeror (1:14). Better no sacrifices at all ("shut the temple door") than blemished sacrifices such as these.

Yahweh declares these sacrifices to be "polluted food on my altar" (1:7). By offering them, the priests say that Yahweh's table itself is "polluted" and its "food" is despised (i.e., treated as worthless). The priests treat their responsibility as a burden, which provokes blowing out of air—either labored breathing because of the effort ("puffing") or "snorting" in derision.

Verses 11 and 14 focus on the status of Yahweh's "name among the nations," involving a three-way contrast with the cultic practices of the priests.

Yahweh's name	Not honored/not feared	Great/feared in the nations
Offering/sacrifice	Defiled	Pure
Place	Yahweh's altar/table	in every place

There is much is debate about these worshippers from the nations—see Goswell (2013:629–33) and Synman (2015:69–76) for a summary of views. It either describes worship in Malachi's day (and, if so, who then are these worshippers—pagan worshippers? diaspora Jews? converted Gentiles?) or worship at some future point. The clauses about Yahweh's name in v. 11 and v. 14 are verbless, and the "offering up of smoke" is described with a participle, so it is not clear on grammatical grounds whether the worship is present or future. While I agree with the view that these verses refer to the future worship of Yahweh by the nations (cf. Zech. 8:20-23, 14:16-21), the emphasis of this passage is not on the conversion of the nations per se (contra Baldwin 1972:228–32), but as a rhetorical rebuke against the priests in Malachi's day. In the past, the sins of his people had profaned Yahweh's "great name … among the nations" *[Ezek. 36:23]*, and—by implication—the priests in Malachi's day are continuing to do this, by their defiled offerings. (cf. Weyde 2000:148). Verses 11 and 14 anticipate the future purification of *Israel's* worship, so that it will result in the "fear" and "honouring of" Yahweh's great name among the nations.

In Mal. 2:1-9, the rebuke against the priests broadens beyond their sacrificial malpractice, to their other priestly duties. This passage is an exhortation to change their ways so that Yahweh's "covenant with Levi" (see below) may stand. If the priests do not listen, there will be three consequences (which take the form of a Deuteronomic curse *[Deut. 28:15-20, 59]* and an inversion of the Priestly Blessing *[Num. 6:23-27]*).

Firstly, Yahweh will "curse their blessings." There is debate as to what this means—either the material blessings the priests *receive* for their ministry will be cursed or priestly blessings they *give* will turn into curses, or perhaps both options. Fishbane (1985:332–4) has observed that Mal. 1:6-2:9 is an ironic reversal of the priestly blessing in Num. 6:24-27, which gives weight to the second option.

The second consequence can be interpreted in different ways, which is further compounded by the LXX (cf. Vulgate), which reads "I will separate the arm" compared to the MT "I will rebuke your seed." The LXX would seem to have arising from mistakenly vocalizing the consonantal text as *zərōaʿ* ("arm") instead of *zeraʿ* ("seed"). Reading with the MT, the rebuke on their "seed" could either refer to material produce (so Glazier-MacDonald 1987:66–8), or—more likely—their descendants (cf. *[Deut. 28:59]*; Petersen 1995:189, Weyde 2000:159–63), with the implication that their sins threaten the ongoing existing of the priesthood as a hereditary institution.

Thirdly, Yahweh will defile them with the offal of their offerings (2:3)—they will become ritually unfit to serve (Redditt 1995:168).

The purpose of theses judgments on the priesthood is "so that [Yahweh's] covenant with Levi may stand." There is no record of a specific covenant between Yahweh and Levi, and so most commentators look to some combination of *[Exod. 32:25-29, Num. 25:10-13, Deut. 33:8-11, and/or Jer. 33:19-21]* to explain this covenant (see Weyde 2000:176–86; Gibson 2016:101–6). The lexical connections with Num. 25:10-13 are outweighed by the fact that that covenant was specifically for Eleazar the priest and his offspring, rather than the entire Levitical priesthood. The best exposition of the content of the covenant with Levi is not from an amalgamation of these passages, but from Mal. 2:5-7.

Malachi 2:5-7 describe the ideal of the Levitical priesthood (in sharp contrast to the priests in Malachi's day). The priest should fear/reverence Yahweh (2:5), true instruction should be in his mouth (2:6), and he should walk with Yahweh in peace and uprightness (2:6).

These priests had failed at every level—they do not fear Yahweh's name (1:6, 1:14, 2:2), their instruction was corrupt and led people astray, and they have turned from walking in Yahweh's way (2:8-9). These priests have utterly failed to be "messengers of Yahweh of Hosts" (2:7)—cf. Mal. 3:1.

Obedience to the covenant would have resulted in "life and peace" (2:5). Instead, Yahweh will treat them in the same way they have treated his offerings—"despised."

[III] Malachi 2:10-16

In the third disputation, the focus shifts from the covenantal failure of the priests to the covenantal failure of the people, expressed in two forms of marital unfaithfulness—marrying "daughters of a foreign god" and divorce.

As noted in §6.5, Mal. 2:10-12 differs from the pattern of the other speeches, in that it is introduced by a triplex of rhetorical questions ("Have we not all one Father? Has not one God created us? Why then are we faithless to one another, profaning the covenant of our fathers?").

Although there are other views, most take "one Father" to refer to Yahweh (contra Baldwin 1972:237, who suggests Abraham), and "who created us" to refer to Yahweh's creation of the nation of Israel, rather than the creation of all humanity (cf. Deut. 32:6) and "covenant of our fathers" to refer to the Mosaic covenant (rather than the Abrahamic covenant) in particular. As such, all three rhetorical questions emphasize the shared familial identity as Yahweh's covenant people, which underscores the horror of what is happening—"being unfaithful" (*bgd*) each against his brother (contra Assis 2009). The Hebrew term *bgd* is a keyword in this section, occurring in vv. 10, 11, 14, 15, and 16.

The first form of covenant unfaithfulness described is "marrying the daughter of a foreign God" (2:11). Although some argue that this is figurative for idolatry (Petersen 1995:199–200), most see this as referring to intermarriage with non-Israelite women. This is an "abomination" because they are *not* worshippers of the one God, the Father of Israel (cf. Deut. 7:3-4).

The negative consequences—being cut off from the tents of Israel—for the one who does this are clear in Mal. 2:12, notwithstanding the fact that there is no clarity about how to translate the clause 'ēr wǝ'ōneh (lit. "awakening and answering")—see Gibson (2014) for twelve alternatives.

The focus shifts in 2:13-16 to a "second" form of unfaithful dealing—breaching the covenant of marriage (Hugenberger 1998:124–67; contra Glazier-MacDonald 1987:101, who takes it to be the covenant with the nation). Yahweh is the unseen witness of those who have covenanted together in marriage, because of their marital infidelity he longer accepts their offerings because he is "acting as a witness" between them.

Verses 15–16 are notoriously difficult to translate, and in the space available it is not possible to do justice to the issues. The first half of v. 15 is elliptical to the point of obscurity—literally "and not one he made, and a remnant of spirit for him/it, and why one? Seeking seed of God." Although some take the referent of "One" to be Yahweh ("The One [God] made them"),

I take it to be referring to the married couple, alluding to *[Gen. 2:23-24]*—that is, "He made them *one*," because he was seeking "godly offspring" (see further Gibson 2016:125–40).

In v. 16, the subject of the verb *śnʾ* ("hate") is unclear—is it "I (Yahweh) hate divorce" or "the one who hates and divorces"? Also unclear is the connection with the clause "he puts a cover of violence on his garments" with what comes before. Furthermore, there is an evident allusion to the divorce laws in *[Deut. 24:1-4]*, but is Malachi affirming or modifying Deuteronomy 24? For a cross section of the possible interpretations of these verses, compare Hill (1998:243–54), Zehnder (2003), Synman (2015:114–19), and Gibson (2016:140–55). I read v. 16 as saying that the one who hates [his wife] and divorces her is covering his garment with violence. This condemnation of divorce on the basis of hate is not necessarily in conflict with Deuteronomy 24, which allows divorce on the basis of indecency (cf. Gibson 2016:148–55).

Notwithstanding the interpretative challenges, the rhetorical force of the passage is clear. The one who hates and divorces has broken faith (both with their spouse and with Yahweh). God's people must "guard themselves in their sprit" (repeated in 2:15 and 2:16) and not do this.

[IV] Malachi 2:17–3:6

The final three disputations arise from the (apparent) failure of Yahweh to punish the wicked and reward the righteous.

The fourth disputation begins with the declaration that the people have wearied Yahweh with their complaints about the wicked who prosper and with their question "Where is the God of *justice*?" (2:17).

In Mal. 3:1-5, Yahweh promises that day is coming when he will "draw near to them for *justice*" (3:5), which will manifest as judgment on the wicked and fiery purification for his people. In asking for the God of justice, the people do not appreciate what they are asking for.

In preparation for his coming, Yahweh declares, "I will send my messenger who will prepare the way before me" (3:1). In addition to Yahweh and "my messenger," v. 1 also refers to "the Lord" (*ʾādôn*) and "the messenger of the covenant."

The key interpretive difficulty relates to the identity of the messenger of the covenant. The chiasmus in v. 1 (A—The Lord will *come* … B—<u>whom you seek</u>//B'—The messenger of the covenant <u>in whom you delight</u>... A'—He is *coming*) would tend to equate the Lord with the messenger of the covenant, and the fact that the "the Lord" is coming to "his temple" suggests that the Lord is Yahweh. However, this means that Yahweh is also the messenger of the covenant, which seems an unlikely way for Yahweh to refer to himself in the third person. But, in the opposite direction, if the messenger of the covenant is *not* Yahweh, there is a tension created by Mal. 3:2, which describes the day of "his" coming (where the most natural referent of "his" is the messenger of the covenant) in terms one might have expected of Yahweh's coming.

One solution is explaining these tensions as arising from complex redactional growth. For example, Petersen (1995:221) and many others regard Mal. 3:1b-4 as a later insertion, whereas Snyman (2015:130) argues that 3:1a is the later insertion.

For those seeking a coherent interpretation of the text in its final form, there are three main options.

1. The traditional Christian interpretation (e.g., Calvin 1849:568–9), made in light of the NT data, takes this to be a messianic prophecy, which involves three persons: Yahweh, Christ—who is both the Lord and the messenger of the covenant—and "my messenger," who is the human forerunner to Christ's coming.

More recent commentators have tended to collapse the three figures into two. There is general agreement that "the Lord" who comes to his temple is Yahweh, but the key point of disagreement relates to the messenger of the covenant.

2. Some, noting the similarities between the messenger(=angel) of the covenant and the angel bearing Yahweh's name in *[Exod. 23:20-21]*, have concluded that the messenger of the covenant is another name for the Angel of the Lord, who is the mode by which Yahweh reveals himself (e.g., Glazier-MacDonald 1987:130–1, Verhoef 1987:289, Gibson 2016:169).
3. Others (e.g., Petersen 1995:210, Petterson 2015:362) argue that the messenger of the covenant is the same as "my messenger." The tension with Mal. 3:2 is handled in different ways. Petterson argues that Mal. 3:2 refers to Yahweh as the purifier, whereas Petersen (and cf. Weyde 2000:284–91) takes Mal. 3:2 to refer to the messenger of the covenant as the purifier.

At the risk of oversimplification, these three views can be represented thus:

1	Yahweh	Christ = Lord = Messenger of covenant	My messenger
2	Yahweh = Lord = Messenger of covenant		My messenger
3	Yahweh = Lord	Messenger of covenant = my messenger	

Although I am inclined to option 2, the key messages are similar for all three options.

1. The people seek "the God of justice" without realizing that his coming on the Day of Yahweh *[Joel 2:11]* will be a terrifying day of judgment for them, not just for the wicked who prosper.
2. Prior to his coming, Yahweh will send a human messenger—whom he describes as "my messenger"—as a forerunner to prepare the way *[cf. Isa. 40:3]*. This messenger is necessary because the priesthood has utterly failed to be a "messenger of Yahweh" (2:17). The prophet Malachi, whose name means "my messenger," is not the messenger described in Mal. 3:1 (thought is perhaps a foreshadowing of the forerunner). The messenger who is to come is another prophetic figure, identified as Elijah the prophet in Mal. 4:5 [MT 3:23].
3. When Yahweh comes (or when the messenger of the covenant comes, if this is not Yahweh), it will be a day of fiery purification for his people *[cf. Isa. 1:26, Zech. 13:9]*. The purification is focused on the sons of Levi, so that their defiled and unacceptable offerings might be replaced with righteous and pleasing offerings (3:3-4).

There is some debate about whether v. 6 is the commencement of the fifth disputations, or the conclusion to the fourth. On the basis that v. 6 begins with *kî* ("For"), I have taken this to be conclusion to the prior unit. The reason why the wicked have not (yet) been punished is not because of a failure of the "God of justice," but because Yahweh (unlike his faithless people) does not change. He remains committed in covenant faithfulness. Israel is not consumed (lit. "come to an end"), because the steadfast love and mercies of Yahweh do not come to an end *[cf. Lam. 3:22]*.

[V] Malachi 3:7-12

The start of v. 7 is transitional between the conclusion of the fourth disputation and the start of the fifth. Unlike Yahweh, who has been constant in this faithfulness to the covenant (3:6), the people have turned away from the decrees of the covenant (3:7). Echoing his words to an earlier generation,

Yahweh tells them, "Return to me and I will return to you" *[Zech. 1:3]*. They will manifest their return to Yahweh by no longer "robbing God" in their tithes and offerings *[Deut. 12:5-12]*. Reading between the lines, the people's attitude is the corollary of their previous complaint. Just as Yahweh does not punish the wicked, they also assumed he does not reward those who do what the covenant stipulates. Assuming that their obedience was irrelevant, the people have only been bringing in part of the tithe. As a result, they are under a curse for covenant disobedience *[Deuteronomy 28]*. The message of this disputation is that, if they turn back in repentance, then Yahweh will pour out the blessings of the covenant *[Deut. 28:12, cf. 30:1-3, 9-10]*, by opening the windows of heaven *[transforming Gen. 7:11]*.

[VI] Malachi 3:13–4:6 [MT 3:13-24]

The final disputation combines the attitudes critiqued in the previous two disputations; there is no reward for the righteous (it is futile to serve God) and there is no punishment for the wicked (evildoers prosper). Yahweh declares these to be "hard words against me."

From the pattern of previous disputations, we might have expected a condemnation or exhortation to follow, but instead, there is a narrative that describes the response of those who "feared Yahweh" (in contrast to the evildoers of v. 15).

Scholars differ as to whether the "scroll of remembrance" drawn up before Yahweh in v. 16 is a divine register of the Yahweh-fearers (a heavenly "book of life") or a human record drawn up by those who feared Yahweh (see Glazier-MacDonald 1987:220–1, Petersen 1995:222). Either way, there is a profound change in status for those names are listed in the book. They are Yahweh's covenant people ("they will be to me" is an abbreviation of the covenant formula), they are his "treasured possession" *[Exod. 19:5; Deut. 7:6; 14:2; 26:18]* and the recipients his mercy. Verse 18 answers the people's complaint that there is no difference between the righteous and the wicked, anticipating the day of judgment when there will be an obvious distinction between the righteous and the wicked on the day of Yahweh (4:1-3).

Many, perhaps most, scholars regard the final three verses as a later redactional addition (see Weyde 2000:388–93, but see the contra argument in Gibson 2016:215–34). Nonetheless, these verses serve as a fitting climax to the message of the book, while at the same time drawing a line of connection between the final book in the prophetic corpus with the Law (Torah) of Moses, and perhaps also a conclusion to the Book of the Twelve as a whole.

Bibliography

Ackroyd, P. R. 1951. "Studies in the Book of Haggai," *Journal of Jewish Studies*, 2: 163–76.

Ackroyd, P. R. 1952. "The Book of Haggai and Zechariah 1–8," *Journal of Jewish Studies*, 3: 151–6.

Ackroyd, P. R. 1968. *Exile and Restoration: A Study of Hebrew Thought of the Sixth Century BC*. London: SCM Press.

Albertz, R. 2003. *Israel in Exile: The History and Literature of the Sixth Century B.C.E.* Atlanta: SBL.

Albertz, R., J. Nogalski, and J. Wöhrle. 2012. *Perspectives on the Formation of the Book of the Twelve: Methodological Foundations, Redactional Processes, Historical Insights*. Berlin: De Gruyter.

Amsler, S. 1972. "Zacharie Et L'origine De L'apocalyptique." In H. S. Nyberg (ed.), *Congress Volume: Uppsala 1971*. Leiden: Brill, 227–31.

Assis, E. 2007. "To Build or Not to Build: A Dispute between Haggai and His People (Hag 1)," *Zeitschrift für die alttestamentliche Wissenschaft*, 119: 514–27.

Assis, E. 2008. "A Disputed Temple (Haggai 2,1-9)," *Zeitschrift für die alttestamentliche Wissenschaft*, 120: 582–96.

Assis, E. 2009. "Love, Hate and Self-Identity in Malachi: A New Perspective to Mal 1:1-5 and 2:10-16," *Journal of Northwest Semitic Languages*, 35: 109–20.

Assis, E. 2010. "Structure and Meaning in the Book of Malachi." In John Day (ed.), *Prophecy and Prophets in Ancient Israel*. New York: T&T Clark, 354–69.

Baldwin, J. G. 1972. *Haggai, Zechariah, Malachi*. London: Tyndale.

Barstad, H. M. 1996. *The Myth of the Empty Land: A Study in the History and Archaeology of Judah during the "Exilic" Period*. Oslo: Scandinavian University Press.

Bedford, P. R. 2001. *Temple Restoration in Early Achaemenid Judah*. Leiden; Boston: Brill.

Behrens, A. 2002. *Prophetische Visionsschilderungen Im Alten Testament: Sprachliche Eigenarten, Funktion Und Geschichte Einer Gattung*. Munster: Ugarit-Verlag.

Berry, D. K. 1996. "Malachi's Dual Design: The Close of the Canon and What Comes Afterward." In James W. Watts and Paul R. House (eds.), *Forming Prophetic Literature*. Sheffield: Sheffield Academic Press, 269–302.

Beuken, W. A. M. 1967. *Haggai-Sacharja 1–8; Studien Zur Überlieferungsgeschichte Der Frühnachexilischen Prophetie*. Assen: Van Gorcum.

Boda, M. J. 2003. "From Fasts to Feasts: The Literary Function of Zechariah 7–8," *Catholic Biblical Quarterly*, 65: 390–407.

Boda, M. J. 2004. *Haggai, Zechariah*. Grand Rapids, MI: Zondervan.

Boda, M. J. 2006. "Freeing the Burden of Prophecy: Massa and the Legitimacy of Prophecy in Zech 9–14," *Biblica*, 87: 338–57.

Boda, M. J. 2008. "Hoy, Hoy: The Prophetic Origins of the Babylonian Tradition in Zechariah 2:10-17." In M. J. Boda and M. H. Floyd (eds.), *Tradition in Transition*. London: T&T Clark, 171–90.

Boda, M. J. 2012. "Perspectives on Priests in Haggai–Malachi." In Eileen M. Schuller, Jeremy Penner, Ken M. Penner, and Cecilia Wassen (eds.), *Prayer and Poetry in the Dead Sea Scrolls and Related Literature*. Leiden; Boston: Brill, 13–33.

Boda, M. J. 2016. *The Book of Zechariah*. Grand Rapids, MI: Eerdmans.

Boda, M. J. 2017. *Exploring Zechariah*—Volume 2. Atlanta: SBL Press.

Boda, M. J., M. H. Floyd, and C. M. Toffelmire. 2015. *The Book of the Twelve and the New Form Criticism*. Atlanta: SBL Press.

Bosshard, E., and R. G. Kratz. 1990. "Maleachi im Zwölfprophetenbuch," *Biblische Notizen*, 52: 27–46.

Briant, P. 2002. *From Cyrus to Alexander: A History of the Persian Empire*. Winona Lake, IN: Eisenbrauns.

Butterworth, M. 1992. *Structure and the Book of Zechariah*. Sheffield: JSOT Press.

Calvin, J. 1849. *Commentaries on the Twelve Minor Prophets—Volume V: Zechariah and Malachi*. Edinb: Calvin Translation Society.

Carter, C. E. 1999. *The Emergence of Yehud in the Persian Period: A Social and Demographic Study*. Sheffield: Sheffield Academic Press.

Childs, B. S. 1979. *Introduction to the Old Testament as Scripture*. London: SCM Press.

Coggins, R. J. 1987. *Haggai, Zechariah, Malachi*. Sheffield: JSOT for the Society for Old Testament Study.

Collins, J. J. 1979. "The Jewish Apocalypses," *Semeia*, 14: 21–59.

Collins, J. J. 2003. "The Eschatology of Zechariah." In Lester L. Grabbe and Robert D. Haak (eds.), *Knowing the End from the Beginning: The Prophetic, the Apocalyptic and Their Relationships*. London: T&T Clark, 74–84.

Conrad, E. W. 1999. *Zechariah*. Sheffield: Sheffield Academic Press.

Cook, S. L. 1995. *Prophecy & Apocalypticism: The Postexilic Social Setting*. Minneapolis: Fortress Press.

Cross, F. M. 1973. *Canaanite Myth and Hebrew Epic: Essays in the History of the Religion of Israel*. Cambridge, MA: Harvard University Press.

Davies, P. R. 1992. *In Search of "Ancient Israel"*. Sheffield: JSOT Press.

Davies, P. R. 1998. *Scribes and Schools: The Canonization of the Hebrew Scriptures*. Louisville, KY: Westminster John Knox Press.

Delcor, M. 1952. "Les Sources Du Deutero-Zacharie Et Ses Procedes D'emprunt," *Revue biblique*, 59: 385–411.

Delkurt, H. 2000. *Sacharjas Nachtgesichte: Zur Aufnahme Und Abwandlung Prophetischer Traditionen*. Berlin: De Gruyter.

Edelman, D. V. 2003. "Proving Yahweh Killed His Wife (Zechariah 5:5-11)," *Biblical Interpretation*, 11: 335–44.

Edelman, D. V. 2005. *The Origins of the "Second" Temple: Persian Imperial Policy and the Rebuilding of Jerusalem*. London: Equinox.

Ego, B., A. Lange, H. Lichtenberger, and K. De Troyer. 2005. *Biblia Qumranica Vol. 3b Minor Prophets*. Leiden: Brill.

Elliger, K., and A. Weiser. 1963. *Das Buch Der Zwölf Kleinen Propheten*. Göttingen: Vandenhoeck & Ruprecht.

Fishbane, M. A. 1985. *Biblical Interpretation in Ancient Israel*. Oxford: Clarendon Press.

Floyd, M. H. 1995. "The Nature of the Narrative and the Evidence of Redaction in Haggai," *Vetus Testamentum*, 45: 470–90.

Floyd, M. H. 2000. *Minor Prophets*. Grand Rapids: Eerdmans.

Floyd, M. H. 2002. "The מַשָּׂא (*maśśā*) as a Type of Prophetic Book," *Journal of Biblical Literature*, 121: 401–22.

Fuller, R. 1991. "Text-Critical Problems in Malachi 2:10-16," *Journal of Biblical Literature*, 110: 47–57.

Galling, K. 1964. "Die Exilswende in Der Sicht Des Propheten Sacharja." In Kurt Galling (ed.), *Studien Zur Geschichte Israels Im Persischen Zeitalter*. Tubingen: Mohr, 109–26.

Gelston, A., and A. Schenker. 2010. *BHQ—The Twelve Minor Prophets*. Stuttgart: Deutsche Bibelgesellschaft.

Gese, H. 1973. "Anfang Und Ende Der Apokalyptik, Dargestellt Am Sacharjabuch," *Zeitschrift für Theologie und Kirche*, 70: 20–49.

Gibson, J. 2014. "Cutting Off 'Kith and Kin,' 'Er and Onan'?: Interpreting an Obscure Phrase in Malachi 2:12," *Journal of Biblical Literature*, 133: 519–37.

Gibson, J. 2016. *Covenant Continuity and Fidelity: A Study of Inner-Biblical Allusion and Exegesis in Malachi*. London: Bloomsbury.

Glazier-MacDonald, B. 1987. *Malachi, the Divine Messenger*. Atlanta: Scholars Press.

Gonzalez, H. 2013. "Zechariah 9–14 and the Continuation of Zechariah during the Ptolemaic Period," *The Journal of Hebrew Scriptures*, 13: Art 9.

Gordon, R. P. 1994. *Studies in the Targum to the Twelve Prophets, from Nahum to Malachi*. Leiden: Brill.

Goshen-Gottstein, M. H. 1983. "The Textual Criticism of the Old Testament: Rise, Decline, Rebirth," *Journal of Biblical Literature*, 102: 365–99.

Goswell, G. 2013. "The Eschatology of Malachi after Zechariah 14," *Journal of Biblical Literature*, 132: 625–38.

Grabbe, L. L. 1995. *Priests, Prophets, Diviners, Sages: A Socio-Historical Study of Religious Specialists in Ancient Israel*. Valley Forge, PA: Trinity Press International.

Grabbe, L. L. 2004. *A History of the Jews and Judaism in the Second Temple Period. Volume 1, Yehud: A History of the Persian Province of Judah*. London: T&T Clark.

Grabbe, L. L. 2006. "The 'Persian Documents' in the Book of Ezra: Are They Authentic?" In Oded Lipschitz and Manfred Oeming (eds.), *Judah and the Judeans in the Persian Period*. Winona Lake, IN: Eisenbrauns, 531–70.

Grabbe, L. L. 2015. "The Reality of the Return: The Biblical Picture versus Historical Reconstruction." In Jonathan Stökl and Caroline Waerzeggers (eds.), *Exile and Return: The Babylonian Context*. Berlin: De Gruyter, 292–307.

Grabbe, L. L. 2016. "The Priesthood in the Persian Period: Haggai, Zechariah, and Malachi." In Lena-Sofia Tiemeyer and Jutta Krispenz (eds.), *Priests and Cults in the Book of the Twelve*. Atlanta: SBL Press, 149–56.

Hallaschka, M. 2011. *Haggai Und Sacharja 1–8: Eine Redaktionsgeschichtliche Untersuchung*. Berlin: De Gruyter.

Hallaschka, M. 2012. "From Cores to Corpus: Considering the Formation of Haggai and Zechariah 1–8." In Rainer Albertz, James Nogalski, and Jakob Wöhrle (eds.), *Perspectives on the Formation of the Book of the Twelve*. Berlin: De Gruyter, 171–90.

Hanson, P. D. 1979. *The Dawn of Apocalyptic: The Historical and Sociological Roots of Jewish Apocalyptic Eschatology*. Philadelphia: Fortress Press.

Harvey, J. 1967. *Le Plaidoyer Prophétique Contre Israël Aprés La Rupture De L'alliance*. Bruges, Paris: Desclee de Brouwer.

Hill, A. E. 1983. "Dating the Book of Malachi: A Linguistic Reexamination." In C. L. Meyers and M. P. O'Connor (eds.), *The Word of the Lord Shall Go Forth*. Winona Lake, IN: Eisenbrauns, 77–89.

Hill, A. E. 1998. *Malachi: A New Translation with Introduction and Commentary*. New York; London: Doubleday.

Hill, A. E. 2012. *Haggai, Zechariah and Malachi: An Introduction and Commentary*. Downers Grove, IL: IVP Academic.

House, P. R. 1992. *Beyond Form Criticism: Essays in Old Testament Literary Criticism*. Winona Lake, IN: Eisenbrauns.

Hugenberger, G. P. 1998. *Marriage as a Covenant: Biblical Law and Ethics as Developed from Malachi*. Grand Rapids, MI: Baker Books.

Hurvitz, A. 2000. "Can Biblical Texts Be Dated Linguistically?: Chronological Perspectives in the Historical Study of Biblical Hebrew." In André Lemaire and Magne Sæbø (eds.), *Congress Volume: Oslo 1998*. Leiden: Brill, 143–60.

Jacobs, M. R. 2017. *The Books of Haggai and Malachi*. Grand Rapids, MI: Eerdmans.

Jansma, T. 1950. "Inquiry into the Hebrew Text and the Ancient Versions of Zechariah IX–XIV." In P. A. H. De Boer (ed.), *Oudtestamentische Studiën*. Leiden: Brill, 1–142.

Jeremias, C. 1977. *Die Nachtgesichte Des Sacharja: Untersuchungen Zu Ihrer Stellung Im Zusammenhang Der Visionsberichte Im Alten Testament Und Zu Ihrem Bildmaterial*. Gottingen: Vandenhoek & Ruprecht.

Jones, D. R. 1962. *Haggai, Zechariah, and Malachi : Introduction and Commentary*. London: SCM Press.

Kasher, R. 2009. "Haggai and Ezekiel: The Complicated Relations between the Two Prophets," *Vetus testamentum*, 59: 556–582.

Keil, C. F. 1961. *The Twelve Minor Prophets*. Grand Rapids, MI: Eerdmans.

Kessler, J. 2002. *The Book of Haggai: Prophecy and Society in Early Persian Yehud*. Leiden: Brill.

Koopmans, W. T. 2017. *Haggai*. Leuven: Peeters.

Lamarche, P. 1961. *Zacharie IX–XIV: Structure Littéraire et Messianisme*. Paris: J. Gabalda.

Larkin, K. J. A. 1994. *The Eschatology of Second Zechariah: A Study of the Formation of a Mantological Wisdom Anthology*. Kampen: Kok.

Lee, S. Y. 2015. *An Intertexual Analysis of Zechariah 9–10: The Earlier Restoration Expectations of Second Zechariah*. New York: Bloomsbury.

Lemche, N. P. 1993. "The Old Testament–A Hellenistic Book?" *Scandinavian Journal of the Old Testament*, 7: 163–93.

Love, M. C. 1999. *The Evasive Text: Zechariah 1–8 and the Frustrated Reader*. Sheffield: Sheffield Academic Press.

Lutz, H.-M. 1968. *Jahwe, Jerusalem Und Die Völker; Zur Vorgeschichte Von Sach. 12, 1–8, Und 14, 1–5*. Neukirchen-Vluyn: Neukirchener Verlag des Erziehungsvereins.

Mason R. A. 1973, "The Use of Earlier Biblical Material in Zechariah IX–XIV: A Study in Inner Biblical Exegesis." PhD diss., University of London. (reprinted as Mason 2003)

Mason, R. A. 1976. "The Relation of Zech. 9–14 to Proto-Zechariah," *Zeitschrift für die alttestamentliche Wissenschaft*, 88: 227–39.

Mason, R. A. 1977. *The Books of Haggai, Zechariah and Malachi*. London: Cambridge University Press.

Mason, R. A. 1982. "The Prophets of the Restoration." In R. J. Coggins, Anthony Phillips, and Michael A. Knibb (eds.), *Israel's Prophetic Tradition*. Cambridge: Cambridge University Press, 137–54.

Mason, R. A. 1990. *Preaching the Tradition: Homily and Hermeneutics after the Exile*. Cambridge: Cambridge University Press.

Mason R. A. 2003. "The Use of Earlier Biblical Material in Zechariah 9–14: A Study in InnerBiblical Exegesis." In M. J. Boda and M. H. Floyd, *Bringing out the Treasure:Inner Biblical Allusion and Zechariah 9-14*. Sheffield: Sheffield Academic,1–208.

Merrill, E. H. 1994. *Haggai, Zechariah, Malachi: An Exegetical Commentary*. Chicago: Moody.

Meyer, L. V. 1977. "Allegory Concerning the Monarchy: Zech 11:4-17; 13:7-9." In Arthur L. Merrill and Thomas W. Overholt (eds.), *Scripture in History and Theology*. Pittsburgh: Pickwick Pr, 225–40.

Meyers, C. L., and E. M. Meyers. 1987. *Haggai, Zechariah 1–8: A New Translation with Introduction and Commentary*. Garden City, NY: Doubleday.

Meyers, C. L., and E. M. Meyers. 1993. *Zechariah 9–14: A New Translation with Introduction and Commentary*. New York: Doubleday.

Middlemas, J. 2011. "The Shape of Things to Come: Redaction and the Early Second Temple Period Prophetic Tradition." In Lester L. Grabbe and Martti Nissinen (eds.), *Constructs of Prophecy in the Former and Latter Prophets and Other Texts*. Atlanta: Society of Biblical Literature, 141–56.

Mitchell, H. G. 1912. *A Critical and Exegetical Commentary on Haggai and Zechariah*. Edinburgh: T&T Clark.

Muilenburg, J. 1969. "Form Criticism and Beyond," *Journal of Biblical Literature*, 88: 1–18.

Niditch, S. 1983. *The Symbolic Vision in Biblical Tradition*. Chico, CA: Scholars Press.

Nogalski, J., and M. A. Sweeney. 2000. *Reading and Hearing the Book of the Twelve*. Atlanta: SBL Press.

Nogalski, J. D. 1993a. *Literary Precursors to the Book of the Twelve*. Berlin: De Gruyter.

Nogalski, J. D. 1993b. *Redactional Processes in the Book of the Twelve*. Berlin: De Gruyter.

Nogalski, J. D. 1996. "Intertextuality and the Twelve." In James W. Watts and Paul R. House (eds.), *Forming Prophetic Literature*. Sheffield: Sheffield Academic Press, 102–24.

Nogalski, J. D. 2011. *The Book of the Twelve: Micah–Malachi*. Macon, GA: Smyth & Helwys.

Nogalski, J. D. 2020. "The Completion of the Book of the Twelve." In Lena-Sofia Tiemeyer and Jakob Wöhrle (eds.), *The Book of the Twelve: Composition, Reception, and Interpretation*. Leiden; Boston: Brill, 65–89.

North, R. 1972. "Prophecy to Apocalyptic Via Zechariah." In H. S. Nyberg (ed.), *Congress Volume, Uppsala, 1971*. Leiden: Brill, 47–71.

Nurmela, R. 1996. *Prophets in Dialogue: Inner-Biblical Allusions in Zechariah 1–8 and 9–14*. Åbo: Åbo Akademi University Press.

O'Brien, J. M. 1990. *Priest and Levite in Malachi*. Atlanta, GA: SBL Press.

Oesterley, W. O. E. 1932. A History of Israel: Volume II. Oxford, Clarendon Press.

Patrick, F. Y. 2008. "Time and Tradition in the Book of Haggai." In Mark J. Boda and Michael H. Floyd (eds.), *Tradition in Transition: Haggai and Zechariah 1–8 in the Trajectory of Hebrew Theology*. New York: T&TClark, 40–55.

Person, R. F. J. 1991. *Deuteronomic Redaction in the Postexilic Period: A Study of Second Zechariah*. Sheffield: JSOT Press.

Petersen, D. L. 1977. *Late Israelite Prophecy: Studies in Deutero-Prophetic Literature and in Chronicles*. Missoula, MT: Published by Scholars Press for SBL.

Petersen, D. L. 1984. *Haggai and Zechariah 1–8: A Commentary*. London: Westminster.

Petersen, D. L. 1995. *Zechariah 9–14 and Malachi: A Commentary*. Louisville, KY: Westminster John Knox Press.

Petersen, D. L. 2003. "Zechariah 9–14: Methodological Reflections." In M. J. Boda and M. H. Floyd (eds.), *Bringing Out the Treasure: Inner Biblical Allusion and Zechariah 9–14*. Sheffield: Sheffield Academic, 210–24.

Petitjean, A. 1969. *Les Oracles Du Proto-Zacharie: Un Programme De Restauration Pour La Communauté Juive Après L'exil*. Louvain: Éditions Impr. orientaliste.

Petterson, A. R. 2009. *Behold Your King: The Hope for the House of David in the Book of Zechariah*. London: T&T Clark.

Petterson, A. R. 2014. "The Flying Scroll That Will Not Acquit the Guilty: Exodus 34.7 in Zechariah 5.3," *Journal for the Study of the Old Testament*, 38: 347–61.

Petterson, A. R. 2015. *Haggai, Zechariah & Malachi*. Nottingham: Apollos.

Pfeiffer, E. 1959. "Die Disputationsworte Im Buche Maleachi: Ein Beitrag Zur Formgeschichtlichen Struktur," *Evangelische Theologie*, 19: 546–68.

Plöger, O. 1968. *Theocracy and Eschatology*. Oxford: Blackwell.

Pola, T. 2003. *Das Priestertum Bei Sacharja: Historische Und Traditionsgeschichtliche Untersuchung Zur Frühnachexilischen Herrschererwartung*. Tübingen: Mohr Siebeck.

Polzin, R. M. 1976. *Late Biblical Hebrew: Toward an Historical Typology of Biblical Hebrew Prose*. Missoula: Scholars Press for Harvard Semitic Museum.

Rainey, A. F. 1969. "The Satrapy 'Beyond the River'," *Australian Journal of Biblical Archaeology*, 1: 51–78.

Redditt, P. L. 1992. "Zerubbabel, Joshua, and the Night Visions of Zechariah," *Catholic Biblical Quarterly*, 54: 249–59.

Redditt, P. L. 1993. "The Two Shepherds in Zechariah 11:4–17." Catholic Biblical Quarterly 55: 676–686.

Redditt, P. L. 1994. "The Book of Malachi in Its Social Setting," *The Catholic Biblical Quarterly*, 56: 240–55.

Redditt, P. L. 1995. *Haggai, Zechariah and Malachi*. Grand Rapids, MI: Eerdmans.

Redditt, P. L. 2000. "The God Who Loves and Hates." In Paul L. Redditt and David Penchansky (eds.), *Shall Not the Judge of All the Earth Do What Is Right?*. Winona Lake, IN: Eisenbrauns, 175–90.

Redditt, P. L. 2003. "The Formation of the Book of the Twelve: A Review of Research." In Paul L. Redditt and Aaron Schart (eds.), *Thematic Threads in the Book of the Twelve*. Berlin: De Gruyter, 1–27.

Redditt, P. L. 2012a. "Redactional Connectors in Zechariah 9–14." In Rainer Albertz, James Nogalski, and Jakob Wöhrle (eds.), *Perspectives on the Formation of the Book of the Twelve*. Berlin: De Gruyter, 207–22.

Redditt, P. L. 2012b. *Zechariah 9–14*. Stuttgart: W. Kohlhammer.

Redditt, P. L. 2015. "Form Criticism in Haggai, Zechariah, and Malachi: From Oral Sayings to Literature." In Mark J. Boda, Michael H. Floyd, and Colin M. Toffelmire (eds.), *The Book of the Twelve and the New Form Criticism*. Atlanta: SBL Press, 265–84.

Redditt, P. L. 2016. "King, Priest, and Temple in Haggai–Zechariah–Malachi and Ezra–Nehemiah." In Lena-Sofia Tiemeyer and Jutta Krispenz (eds.), *Priests and Cults in the Book of the Twelve*. Atlanta: SBL Press, 157–72.

Redditt, P. L., and A. Schart. 2003. *Thematic Threads in the Book of the Twelve*. Berlin: De Gruyter.

Reventlow, H. G. 1993. *Die Propheten Haggai, Sacharja Und Maleachi Rev. Ed.* Gottingen: Vandenhoeck & Ruprecht.

Rose, W. H. 2000. *Zemah and Zerubbabel: Messianic Expectations in the Early Postexilic Period*. Sheffield: Sheffield Academic Press.

Rost, L. 1951. "Bemerkungen Zu Sacharja 4," *Zeitschrift für die alttestamentliche Wissenschaft*, 63: 216–21.

Rudolph, W. 1976. *Haggai, Sacharja 1–8, Sacharja 9–14, Maleachi*. Gütersloh: Gütersloher Verlagshaus Mohn.

Schaefer, K. R. 1995. "Zechariah 14: A Study in Allusion," *Catholic Biblical Quarterly*, 57: 66–91.

Schniedewind, W. M. 2004. *How the Bible Became a Book: The Textualization of Ancient Israel*. Cambridge: Cambridge University Press.

Schöttler, H. G. 1987. *Gott Inmitten Seines Volkes: Die Neuordnung Des Gottesvolkes Nach Sacharja 1–6*. Trier: Paulinus-Verlag.

Shin, S.-Y. 2016. "A Diachronic Study of the Language of Haggai, Zechariah, and Malachi," *Journal of Biblical Literature*, 135: 265–81.

Silverman, J. M. 2015. "Sheshbazzar, a Judean or a Babylonian? A Note on His Identity." In Jonathan Stökl and Caroline Waerzeggers (eds.), *Exile and Return: The Babylonian Context*. Berlin: De Gruyter, 308–21.

Smith, J. M. P. 1912. *A Critical and Exegetical Commentary on the Book of Malachi*. Edinburgh: T&T Clark.

Snyman, F. 2015. *Malachi*. Leuven: Peeters.

Stade, B. 1881. "Deuterozacharja: Eine Kritische Studie," *Zeitschrift für die alttestamentliche Wissenschaft*, 1: 1–96.

Stade, B. 1882a. "Deuterozacharja: Eine Kritische Studie," *Zeitschrift für die alttestamentliche Wissenschaft*, 2: 151–72.

Stade, B. 1882b. "Deuterozacharja: Eine Kritische Studie," *Zeitschrift für die alttestamentliche Wissenschaft*, 2: 275–309.

Stead, M. R. 2009. *The Intertextuality of Zechariah 1–8*. London, New York: T&T Clark.

Stead, M. R. 2011. "The Three Shepherds: Reading Zechariah 11 in the Light of Jeremiah." In J. A. Grant, A. Lo, and G. J. Wenham (eds.), *A God of Faithfulness*. New York: T&T Clark, 149–65.

Stead, M. R. 2012. "Visions, Prophetic." In Mark J. Boda and J. G. McConville (eds.), *Dictionary of the Old Testament Prophets*. Downers Grove, IL: IVP Academic, 818–26.

Stead, M. R. 2013. "Suffering David, Suffering Servant, Stricken Shepherd." In M. R. Stead (ed.), *Christ Died for Our Sins: Essays on the Atonement*. Canberra: Barton Books, 59–79.

Stead, M. R. 2014. "The Interrelationship between Vision and Oracle in Zechariah 1-6." In E. R. Hayes and L.-S. Tiemeyer (eds.), *"I Lifted my Eyes and Saw": Reading Dream and Vision Reports in the Hebrew Bible*. London: T & T Clark, 149–168.

Steck, O. H. 1991. *Studien Zu Tritojesaja*. Berlin: De Gruyter.

Sweeney, M. A. 2000. *The Twelve Prophets: Micah, Nahum, Habakkuk, Zephaniah, Haggai, Zechariah, Malachi*. Collegeville, MI: Liturgical Press.

Tai, N. H. F. 1996. *Prophetie Als Schriftauslegung in Sacharja 9–14: Traditions- Und Kompositionsgeschichtliche Studien*. Stuttgart: Calwer.

Tiemeyer, L.-S. 2004. "Compelled by Honour–A New Interpretation of Zechariah ii 12a (8a)," *Vetus Testamentum*, 54: 352–72.

Tiemeyer, L.-S. 2006. "A Busy Night at the Heavenly Court," *Svensk Exegetisk Årsbok*, 71: 187–207.

Tiemeyer, L.-S. 2016. *Zechariah's Vision Report and Its Earliest Interpreters: A Redaction-Critical Study of Zechariah 1–8*. New York: Bloomsbury T&T Clark.

Tiemeyer, L.-S. 2019. "Dating Zechariah 1–8: The Evidence in Favour of and against Understanding Zechariah 3 and 4 as Sixth Century Texts." In Richard J. Bautch and Mark Lackowski (eds.), *On Dating Biblical Texts to the Persian Period*. Tübingen: Mohr Siebeck, 65–78.

Tiemeyer, L.-S. 2020. "The Haggai–Zechariah 1–8 Corpus." In Lena-Sofia Tiemeyer and Jakob Wöhrle (eds.), *The Book of the Twelve: Composition, Reception, and Interpretation*. Leiden: Brill, 38–64.

Tollington, J. A. 1993. *Tradition and Innovation in Haggai and Zechariah 1–8*. Sheffield: JSOT Press.

Torrey, C. C. 1936. "The Foundry of the Second Temple at Jerusalem," *Journal of Biblical Literature*, 55: 247–60.

Tov, E. 2001. *Textual Criticism of the Hebrew Bible*. Minneapolis: Fortress Press.

Utzschneider, H. 1989. *Künder Oder Schreiber?: Eine These Zum Problem Der "Schriftprophetei" Auf Grund Von Maleachi 1,6–2,9*. Frankfurt am Main: Peter Lang.

van der Woude, A. S. 1988. "Zion as Primeval Stone in Zechariah 3 and 4." In W. Claassen (ed.), *Text and Context*. Sheffield: JSOT Press, 237–48.

VanderKam, J. C. 1991. "Joshua the High Priest and the Interpretation of Zechariah 3," *Catholic Biblical Quarterly*, 53: 553–70.

Verhoef, P. A. 1987. *The Books of Haggai and Malachi*. Grand Rapids MI: Eerdmans.

Webb, B. G. 2003. *The Message of Zechariah*. Leicester: IVP.

Wellhausen, J. 1885. *Prolegomena to the History of Israel*. Edinburgh: Black.

Wellhausen, J. 1957. *Prolegomena to the History of Israel*. New York: Meridian.

Wenzel, H. 2011. *Reading Zechariah with Zechariah 1:1-6 as the Introduction to the Entire Book*. Leuven; Walpole, MA: Peeters.

Wenzel, H. 2018. *The Book of the Twelve: An Anthology of Prophetic Books or the Result of Complex Redactional Processes?*. Osnabruck: Universitätsverlag Osnabrück/V&R unipress.

Wessels, W. 2005. "Bridging the Gap: Haggai's Use of Tradition to Secure the Future," *Old Testament Essays*, 18: 426–43.

Weyde, K. W. 2000. *Prophecy and Teaching: Prophetic Authority, Form Problems, and the Use of Traditions in the Book of Malachi*. Berlin: De Gruyter.

Weyde, K. W. 2018. "'Once Again the Term maśśā' in Zechariah 9:1; 12:1 and in Malachi 1:1: What Is Its Significance?" *Acta Theologica*, 26: 251–67.

Willi-Plein, I. 1974. *Prophetie Am Ende: Untersuchungen Zu Sacharja 9–14*. Köln: Hanstein.

Williamson, H. G. M. 1983. "The Composition of Ezra 1–6," *The Journal of Theological Studies*, 34: 1–30.

Williamson, H. G. M. 1985. *Ezra, Nehemiah*. Waco: Word.

Wöhrle, J. 2006a. *Die Frühen Sammlungen Des Zwölfprophetenbuches: Entstehung Und Komposition*. Berlin: De Gruyter.

Wöhrle, J. 2006b. "The Formation and Intention of the Haggai–Zechariah Corpus," *Journal of Hebrew Scriptures*, 6: Article 10.

Wöhrle, J. 2016. "On the Way to Hierocracy: Secular and Priestly Rule in the Books of Haggai and Zechariah." In Lena-Sofia Tiemeyer and Jutta Krispenz (eds.), *Priests and Cults in the Book of the Twelve*. Atlanta, GA: SBL Press, 173–90.

Wolff, H. W. 1988. *Haggai: A Commentary*. Minneapolis: Augsburg.

Wolters, A. M. 2008. "'The Whole Earth Remains at Peace' (Zechariah 1:11): The Problem and an Intertextual Clue." In M. J. Boda and M. H. Floyd (eds.), *Tradition in Transition*. London: T. & T. Clark, 128–43.

Wolters, A. M. 2014. *Zechariah*. Leuven: Peeters.

Yamauchi, E. M. 1980. "The Reverse Order of Ezra/Nehemiah Reconsidered," *Themelios*, 5(3): 7–13.

Young, I., R. Rezetko, and M. Ehrensvärd. 2008. *Linguistic Dating of Biblical Texts*. London; Oakville, CT: Equinox Pub.

Zehnder, M. 2003. "A Fresh Look at Malachi ii 13-16," *Vetus Testamentum*, 53: 224–59.

Author Index

Scripture Index

9:13-15	86	12:6	92
9:14-16	83	12:7	92
9:15	92	12:8	86
9:16	65	12:9	70
9:16-17	68, 86	12:9-14	92
10-11	63	12:10	92, 93, 94
10:1-2	67, 94	12:10-13:1	66
10:1-3	88	12:11	61
10:1-4	87	12:12-14	93, 94
10:1-12	66, 68	13:1	70, 94
10:2-3	66, 68, 91	13:2	70
10:2-11	68	13:2-6	13, 66, 94
10:3-11	77	13:3	71, 77
10:3-11:3	65, 66	13:4	70
10:5-12	87	13:6	72, 77, 79
10:6	92	13:7-9	66, 67, 70, 95
10:6-12	65	13:9	118
10:6b+9a	96	14	65
10:8	88	14:1	91
10:10-11	88	14:1-5	96
10:12	64	14:1-15	66
11	63, 88	14:1-21	66, 67, 69, 70
11:1-3	66, 67, 88	14:2	64
11:2	64, 88	14:4	97
11:4	79, 90	14:6	64
11:4-17	66, 89, 67, 91	14:6-7	97
11:4-13:9	65	14:8-12	97
11:7	11, 64, 90	14:10-11	97
11:10-14	90	14:13-21	97, 98
11:11	65	14:14	65
11:11-13	91	14:16-21	66, 113
11:12	63	14:20-21	98
11:13	61, 63	14:21	65, 90
11:15-17	89, 91		
11:17	67	Mal.	
12:1	65, 75, 96, 104	1:1	101
12:1-13:6	66	1:1	106
12:1-2	70, 92	1:1-5	108, 110, 111
12:1-9	66, 67	1:2-4	102
12:1a	65	1:2-5	105, 106
12:1a-13:9	69	1:5	112
12:2-7	65	1:6	14, 114
12:3	70	1:6-2:9	64, 105, 106, 108,
12:3-8	92		110, 112, 114